My Little Blue Tattoo

By
Gershon G. Ron

First edition

My Little Blue Tattoo
By
Gershon G. Ron

Published by AFDP-Publishing
Plymouth, MA 02360 U.S.A.
www.AFDP-Publishing.com
Admin@AFDP-Publishing.com

Title by Bob Shapiro
Cover photo by Odie Ron.
Back cover photo by Margaret McCarthy

Printed in the United States of America

Copyright © 2006

ISBN, Print edition 0-9772434-3-5

DEDICATION

I wish to dedicate this book to the six million Jews who perished in ghettoes and concentration camps during World War II.

ACKNOWLEDGEMENT

I want to thank all those who read my manuscript and thought enough of it to encourage me to publish it. Special thanks to Dr. Aaron Greenwald for his editing, and to Judy Shiner for going over the first draft. My many thanks to Mr. John Lundgren for his supportive letter that is reprinted on the final two pages. Many thanks to my childhood friend, Zoli Berkovic (Meir Barak), for authenticating many stories.

To MR. GEORGE MASON

THERE ARE OCCURRENCES THAT
ETCHES DEEP IMPRESSIONS IN ONES
LIFE; I AM LOST FOR WORDS!
THANK YOU!

FLEISCHMANNS 10/03/2007

IN THE BEGINNING

In the beginning. Whatever!

I began in Zdana, a small village in southern Slovakia, six miles south of Kosice or Kassa or Kassau, the second largest city in Slovakia

Strange isn't it, that Kosice, a small city of 70,000 inhabitants, should have so many names? Not to be left out, Zdana also had a second name. The Hungarians named it Hernadzsadany. More appropriate, because the Hornad River flows on its eastern border.

So how come all this names?

First, Slovakia didn't exist until 1939. Before World War I it belonged to the Austro-Hungarian Empire. Czechoslovakia was created in 1918, after the end of the war. It lasted only 20 years. In 1938, the Hungarian army occupied the southern part of Slovakia after the Munich Treaty sell out by British Prime Minister Sir Neville Chamberlain, to Third Reich Fuhrer Adolf Hitler. The northern part became the independent Slovakia under the rule of Fascist Prime Minister Dr. Tisso. In March 1944, the German army occupied the territory we lived in, and we became subjects of the Third Reich. Czechoslovakia was recreated following World War II, but after a short time, Slovakia broke from the union and became the Slovak Republic.

This should clear up the confusion of different names. The village of Zdana had two streets. One headed to the south, the other turned west at the village square. It didn't matter in which direction you went. Both ended on the Hungarian border. The roads were not paved; the houses had no running water, no gas, no electricity, no telephone, no radio, and no toilets. The only running water was in the Hornad River, and the brook bordering my aunt and uncle Rauchmann's house.

The floors in the houses were of red clay, and the roofs were covered with straw. Every time a lightning struck, the houses caught fire. All the villagers ran with pails of water to put out the fires. Most of the time they succeeded before the horse drawn fire engine arrived.

That is the environment I was born into without my consent. I was robbed of my "Free Will." Was I asked to be born? Certainly not! If I had been asked, would I have agreed to be born in Zdana? Certainly not! Did I will my parents to bear me?

Certainly not!

My father was 33 years old when he married my mother, who was 25. So what was the big hurry? The big depression was looming. How smart was it to bring a child into this cruel world without consulting the one who would have to face the music?

So much for Free Will!

I hardly got used to the surroundings, when, to my great surprise, I was confronted with the news of my brother's birth. That's all I had dreamed of. A competitor!

I was so annoyed, (I was only three and a half years old) I picked up my pillow and moved to our neighbor, the Schonberger's house across the yard. It took my parents a week to convince me to move back home. They used our maid, Katka to coax me back.

At the time, I was influenced more by Katka Veresova than anybody else. I loved her a lot. On the other hand, the Schonbergers might also have helped. They had eight kids of their own and were probably happy to get rid of me.

My brother was named Andrew Aaron. Aaron was his Hebrew (Aharon) name, after our paternal grandfather. I also had two names. Gabriel Gershon. Gershon was named after my maternal grandfather. The names Gershon and Aaron were never used. They were too Jewish for my family's taste. It didn't really matter. As early as three or four years I found out that for the other, non Jewish, kids in the village, I wasn't Gabriel or, for short, Gabi.

We Jewish kids all had the same name: "Dirty Jew."

Later, at the age of six, when school started for us, those same village kids changed their names for us from "Dirty Jew" to "Christ Killer."

Those little bastards were terribly indoctrinated in their church by their ignorant and anti-Semitic priests, who never missed an opportunity to preach about Jews killing Christ. The priests were Roman Catholic. Of course, it is possible those little bastards didn't need to be indoctrinated. They carried the bug of racism and hatred of Jews in their genes.

2

The kids from Protestant and Evangelical families became our friends. In our village of Zdana, they too, were a minority.

THE HOUSE

The multi purpose house that we owned was on the western part of the village. A stone structure, white washed, with the roof covered with red cement tiles. The rooms were lined up one after the other, connected by doors.

The first room, facing the street, was used as the village country store. A bell hung over the door. When rung, it could be heard a mile away. It rang whenever a customer entered the store. Usually the store was unattended. When my mother heard the bell she took off, like shot from a cannon, and ran to service the customer. The store was open five days a week; closed on Saturday because of the Sabbath, and Sunday because of the blue laws. On Sundays the selling went on behind closed doors, and the business flourished. The smugglers from Hungary bought everything not nailed down or available on their side.

Even though the police station was next door to us, I don't remember them ever having interfered with the smugglers. What was the arrangement between my parents and the police, or between them and the smugglers? I have no idea.

The area of the store, though small, nevertheless offered a variety of items: everything from flour, sugar, salt, kerosene, chocolate, pencils, pens, inkwells, textiles, and many more items. Too many to fill a page.

Next to the store was the master bedroom. It was the only bedroom in the house. We kids slept in the same room with our parents until such suspicions arose that certain noises might be disturbing our sleep. From then on, my brother and I slept in the living room. Next was the kitchen. Not like any other. Our kitchen was a multi-purpose room. It served as a dining room, playroom, bakery, and our maid, Katka's, divan was stuck in one corner.

The oddest use of the kitchen was when it was converted into an incubator. Boxes filled with straw were lined up next to the wall where the little ducklings were hatched. The ducks were too impatient to sit on their eggs to hatch. Therefore a large hen was chosen for a

4

substitute. When the little ducks hatched, the hen was sure the ducklings were her offspring. But the ducklings knew better. As soon as they went for a stroll next to the brook, the little yellow things hopped into the water for a swim. The hen got very excited, running up and down on the riverbank, all crazy like, until the ducklings had their fun and returned to their adopted mama.

Next to the kitchen was the living room. The living room contained the best furniture in the house. It was used only to entertain guests. There were two more rooms, separated from the living quarters. One was used for storage and the other was the chicken coop.

In the early stages of my life my parents had bought the house from the Schonbergers. The two buildings faced each other. They created a closed courtyard that eventually became our soccer field.

The back yard was fenced off and became the domain of the chickens, ducks, geese, turkeys, and a crazy dog.

No wonder the dog was crazy. The poor animal was chained day and night. Daytime on a short chain, at night on a long one attached to a cable running between the two buildings.

One day my brother and I were teasing the dog. The dog broke loose and began to chase us. My brother ran to the gate in the fence but I took the wrong turn and ended up in the outhouse. My mother tried to coax the dog away from the outhouse with food, but to no avail. I was stuck there for hours, until my father came home and chained up the dog.

In my eyes, Katka, our maid, was my nanny. She was in her teens when she came to work in our house. She treated me as her child and I reciprocated; loving her. She gave me a piggyback ride every time she went to fetch water at the well. I followed her like a puppy. Wherever she went, I followed. I liked to watch her milk the cows, feed the chickens, the ducks, and force feed the geese in order to grow a huge liver for the famous pate.

Katka saved my life when I was four years old and was ready to hide me when the Nazis were rounding up the Jews. I still think about her often.

THE HEBREW SCHOOL

At the age of three, or maybe four, I was sent to the Hebrew school located in the local synagogue; a stone's throw from our house.

So much for free will!

The room for studies was located at the entrance of the synagogue. It was used for studies in the winter because it had a stove. It was a small room, with only one small window overlooking the yard where the weeds were so high they blocked the sunlight from entering the room. The floor was covered with rutted wooden planks smelling of mildew. The books also smelled. They had a peculiar smell; a mixture of old paper turning yellow mixed with vapor and dust. The teacher, called the Melamed, didn't smell like roses either.

The whole class comprised of five students. There was Zoli, my closest friend, the cantor's three kids: Shaye, Moishe, Chaim, and me.

From the first day, we started to learn the Aleph, Beth (ABC), and to read and write Hebrew. The second item on the agenda was the prayers. We had to memorize prayers for the morning, the afternoon, the evening, and if that wasn't enough, some more for the night. As soon as we mastered one, there came more: the blessings. Blessings for bread, for fruit, for potatoes, for starting a prayer, for ending a prayer, and hundreds more.

I learned every one by rote. I could rattle off any at the right time and in the right sequence with no mistakes. Because mistakes were punishable by going to hell. The prayers were in Hebrew. And because nobody bothered to translate the meanings of the prayers into a language I understood, for every practical purpose, I became a parrot with a capitol P. The time and effort spent learning all those prayers and blessings I could have mastered calculus II.

So much for free will!

By the time I was six or seven, I started to learn the Five Books of Moses. I had to translate from the original Hebrew into

Yiddish. Because I didn't understand Yiddish, I was translating one unknown language into another, and having no idea of what it's all about. The only thing I learned was that God spoke to Moses, then Moses spoke to Aaron, his brother, then Aaron spoke to the people. Or was it the other way? Whatever.

The bubble had to burst somehow somewhere. And it did! On one of those treacherous days, the teacher (the Melamed) stepped outside to relieve himself. I also had the urge.

The outhouse was quit a distance from the classroom. It was verboten to leave the classroom without permission. I started to yell "may I go out" to get the teacher's attention. He probably didn't hear my request and I wasn't going to transgress by leaving the classroom.

At the time, I was translating the word "'v' ani" (and I) but yelling "may I go out" in Hebrew. After a short time I had the two mixed up and was translating the words "and I" to "may I go out"

On Saturday, after the morning prayers we went to the Rabbi's house to be tested on the section we learned. When my turn came and I reached the words "and I" and translated it to "may I go out" The Rabbi was appalled. He thought that in the middle of the test I was trying to leave the room. "What are you talking about?" And I, not realizing what was happening, continued to repeat the lines in a sing-song manner, the way we learned to do it. I didn't suspect that something was wrong until I felt a clop on the back of my head and then another one.

After the test, I returned to the classroom for the payback for embarrassing the teacher. I got a good shellacking.

Nothing changed. We continued to translate from Hebrew into Yiddish. Maybe the Rabbi and the teacher were not interested in being challenged by our questions (I had plenty) and would rather kept us ignorant.

I don't know whether my parents knew about us being mistreated, or they just turned their backs so as not to challenge the authority of the Rabbi and the Melamed.

THE MOSAIC

The front yard of our house was separated from the back by a tall fence. In the left corner of the backyard, next to the manure pile, was the garbage dump. Every spring the manure was disposed of, but the garbage wasn't touched. I was too young to remember when and how I decided to make use of things nobody else wanted; except the chicken that picked at the things on top of the pile, for whatever reason it had. Maybe looking at that chicken, I got the idea that I too, can find something useful on the pile.

I was a small kid, maybe four, when I decided to be a decorator.

The garden was adjacent to the backyard. It was separated by a fence with a narrow opening. The garden was a typical country, provincial type garden, with trees all around the fences. Plum trees, apple trees, pear trees, and peach trees. Also raspberry and blueberry bushes. The rest of the garden was divided into small parcels where all kind of vegetables were grown. Everything from carrots, chives, onions, red and white radishes, potatoes, and you name it.

Since some ideas that pop up into a man's head may be unexplainable, this is one of them. I haven't got an inkling how the idea was born to make a mosaic around the garden fence.

From the garbage pile I began picking up all kinds of colored pieces of bricks, cement tiles, glass, glass bottles that I tried to smash into pieces, and everything that shined. I had about two yards finished when I found the piece de resistance: a broken demijohn. I carried the big piece of glass to the garden where I planned to smash it. As I was juggling it through the narrow opening in the garden fence, I fell and cut my throat on the sharp edge of the broken demijohn.

At the same moment, Katka, our maid, came to fetch water from the well that was only a couple of yards from the garden fence. She grabbed me and started to run up the hill screaming. My mother ran with Katka across the street to the doctor's office. Luckily the cut wasn't deep and the artery wasn't touched. However, it took 18 stitches to close the wound. Dr. Malmos Miksa must have been an excellent surgeon because there is not a trace of the wound.

If I had to have an accident, I couldn't have chosen a better time. Dr. Malmos served not only our village, but the surrounding little hamlets. He was the only doctor and was on call 24 hours a day, seven days a week.

Dr. Malmos just happened to be home and Katka just happened to come to the well to fetch water at the right moment. That's how I was saved.

A conglomeration of circumstances.

CALAMITIES

My friend, Zoli Berkovic, (Meir Barak) told me that as a kid I was full of ideas. Mostly in sports. I don't know how, but one day I came up with the idea to build a pair of skis. I must have seen it somewhere. A kid just doesn't dream up a pair of skis from nowhere.

I got two slats from the fence, two inches wide, by one inch thick. I shaved off the fronts and hammered two nails onto each side of the slats. I took a rope to fasten the shoes to the contraption I called skis. Soon I found two sticks. I was ready to become a downhill skier. I tried to teach my little brother, Andrew, but the slats were to long. He couldn't handle them. I didn't know that skis come in different lengths.

One of my friends found a skate. I don't remember who found the skate and under what circumstances. I do remember it was only one skate. The frozen brook next to my uncle Rauchmann's house became our skating rink. All of our little gang learned how to skate on this one skate. Later, when in high school, I bought a pair of skates. I had no problem adjusting.

As children, we had our calamities. It started with me cutting my neck. My brother broke his left tibia sledding. And I had little scratches here and there. Nothing serious.

One scary moment in our young lives came one winter. My brother and I were in my uncle's house. I went home but my brother stayed to play with our cousin, Ella.

Old Joe, my uncle's father, used to bring people from the railroad station to the village; summer time in a carriage and winter time on a sled. That year, a winter storm blew in from nowhere. Old Joe was ready to bring his sled to the railroad station. Because he had to pass our house, Aunt Kati decided to send my brother home. The distance from their house to ours was less than 200 yards, so it didn't enter Aunt Kati's mind to bundle up my brother. She put him on the back of the sled and off they went. Old Joe forgot that he had a passenger to drop off, and passed our house, with my brother not dressed for the now extended trip.

When my mother found out what happened, she panicked. Notwithstanding the storm, my mother and our maid, Katka, took to the road to look for the kid. Half way to the railroad station, they met the sled returning home with my brother bundled up in the lap of the passengers. It was a happy ending to a trip not planned.

On another occasion, my brother was riding a horse. He forgot to bend down when entering the stable and hit his eye on the facade. His eye swelled and he couldn't see for a long time.

For all these calamities I was blamed. Guilty or not.

Taking in consideration the frequent tree climbing, jumping from trees into the river, sledding, skating, and biking, it was a miracle that we didn't get hurt more often and more seriously.

FAMILY AFFAIR

My father and his partner, Mr. Gross, from the neighboring village of Cana, rented a stone quarry from Baroness Lila Kekedi, who lived on a sprawling estate across the border in Keked, Hungary. The quarry supplied stones to the railroads and for the local roads. Business was good. It got much better because the Czechoslovak government decided to build something similar to the French Maginot Line, so a lot of stones were needed to build the reinforced concrete bunkers.

The available trucks were not equipped to travel off the roads, therefore the partners decided to organize every available horse-drawn wagon to carry the stones to places were trucks couldn't reach. My uncle, Moritz Rauchmann, who was idle at the time, had four horses and two wagons. He joined the army of peasants that the partners hired. Every wagon had to be loaded with one cubic meter of stones. True to the feelings of peasants to their animals, most of them decided to cheat a little bit and load less than was required, to ease the horses' burden. They didn't take into consideration that the load would be measured. My uncle and his father were no different. They too, loaded less than the cubic meter required.

The cheating didn't last for long. The delivered stones were piled up under a triangular contraption that measured the quantity required. The missing amount was recorded and logged. On Friday, the discrepancies were brought to the attention of the peasants and, according to the amount missing, the appropriate sum was deducted from their pay.

When uncle Moritz and his father's sheet were produced, the findings were the same as the rest of the bunch. My father deducted a certain amount, the same as he did with the other peasants. Uncle Moritz took it in stride. He knew that my father had a partner and couldn't make any exceptions.

Not so my father's sister, Kati. She came running. She accused my father of not being fair. Maybe she used some accusations that didn't sit well with my father. He was a very quiet man. I never heard him raise his voice, even in the most trying circumstances. This time he blew his top. Both my father and his sister went ballistic. I never heard such screaming in my life, never in our house and not elsewhere.

We kids had a very close relationship with the Rauchmanns. Uncle Moritz had horses. We hung around for hours just to get a ride, if not more than only from the wagon to the stable. Uncle Moritz was always accommodating, no matter how tired he was. No wonder we loved him.

The relationship between our parents and the Rauchmanns soon soured. Uncle Moritz and his father continued to deliver stones, but the Saturday visits, after prayers, stopped. Those visits were a tradition. The Rauchmanns had to pass our house going home from the synagogue, and all those years they never missed a chance to come in, have a drink and a bite from the Danish pastry my mother used to bake; uncle Moritz's favorite.

Through all this period we kids were welcomed in their house. However, after a while (it had to be a year) the families made up and life went on as before.

Go figure!

THE BARONESS LILA KEKEDI

How can I forget the Baroness Lila Kekedi, the fat lady who appeared every Friday in front of our house?

The quarry that my father and his partner had rented belonged to the Baroness Lila Kekedi. She lived on her estate, across the border in Hungary. I think she was an old maid. The village adjacent to the estate was Keked. No wonder her name was Kekedi. Most of the property belonged to her, not only on the Hungarian side, but also across the border in our Czechoslovakia.

My father and his partner invested a fortune in the quarry. They bought all the equipment necessary for the undertaking. The Baroness was a silent partner, not having to invest a penny.

Every Friday afternoon a horse drawn carriage, pulled by two black steeds, stopped in front of our house. The coachman was dressed in a black uniform with a lot of gold buttons and a top hat, fit for the opera. In the back of the carriage sat the fat lady, dressed in lilac. It was the Baroness Lila Kekedi. Lila is Hungarian for lilac

My father came out of the store, approached the carriage, kissed the fat lady's hand, and handed her a white envelope. It was the weekly share for the partner, who by the grace of kings, owned everything as far as the eye can see.

The carriage, carrying the Baroness, disappeared as fast as it appeared and reappeared equally ceremoniously the following Friday. Was she counting the money on her way home?

As much as I remember, the Baroness never got off her fat ass. She never acknowledged the presence of my mother or us kids. She never came to our house to have tea. I am sure she was invited. I resented her.

I resented my father kissing her hand and bowing in front of this fat pig, the Baroness Lila Kekedi. I wouldn't be surprised that my leaning toward socialism was formed by watching the humiliation my father had to endure from a fat lady like Lila Kekedi!

In October 1938, in accord with the agreement reached in Munich, in which Czechoslovakia was sold out by her allies; France and England, the Hungarian army occupied the territory we lived in. Gone was the democracy we all enjoyed under Presidents Thomas Masaryk and Dr. Edward Benes.

Admiral Miklos Horthy became the new ruler. Immediately, anti Jewish laws were enacted. The Baroness, true to her aristocratic upbringing, canceled the contract with my father's firm. She needed no partners now. The new laws backed her up to the hilt. She didn't have to apologize.

My father and his partner lost most of their income. The only livelihood my parents were left with was the little country store in our house.

It was a year before the outbreak of World War II. My brother and I never felt the crunch. For us, life was as pleasant or as unpleasant as before.

So much for free will!

THE FIST FIGHT

It was a Saturday when two competitors slugged it out in the synagogue. The Berkovics brothers were reasonably well-to-do people. The older brother had a butcher shop in the neighboring village of Misla, and the younger also had a butcher shop in our village; Zdana. The third actor in this story was also a butcher. He had a shop in Nadost, a village less then a mile from Zdana. Because Zdana had the only temple and rabbi, all the Jews from the four neighboring villages came to pray in our synagogue.

So far so good!

The Jewish congregation in Zdana was no different than the rest of the world. There were only 18 Jewish families in the four villages. All were religious, more or less, except the two doctors, Dr. Malmos and Dr. Jonap who were "two day" Jews: Rosh Hashanah and Yom Kippur. The holiday sitting arrangement in the synagogue mirrored the ranking of the members in the Jewish hierarchy of Zdana. The seats on the east side of the synagogue faced the congregation. On the right side sat the rabbi, the synagogue president, and one of the well-to-do members from the village of Nadost. On the left side, facing the congregation, were the Berkovics brothers, my father's uncle, Chaim Roth, and Mr. Levy. He was the owner of a mill in Misla. An explosion in his mill burned his face, and he was badly scarred.

The rest of the congregation set in long benches facing the Ark for the Torah. For reasons unknown to me, the Berkovics and Mermelsteins had a spat. On Saturdays, the last reading of the Torah was always put out for a bid. The bidding was pro forma. The people who got the honor were the ones who had a Yarzeit (memorial), or the Bar-Mitzvah boys. The Saturday in question was the Yarzeit of Mr. Mermelstein. He asked my father, president at the time, to bid for him. My father suspected that the Berkovics brother, for spite, would outbid him.

My father did what was asked, well knowing that Mermelstein was not in a financial position to compete with the Berkovics

16

brothers. At the moment that Mermelstein was called to the Torah, the Berkovics brothers realized the ruse. Both, like shot from a cannon, jumped up from their seats and attacked Mermelstein in front of the open scrolls. The older brother was closing on my father, but Uncle Moritz, a head taller and 50 pounds heavier, stepped between them. Berkovics chose not to challenge him. Smart move, Berkovics!

The fight didn't last long. Mermelstein was bleeding from his nose, Berkovics from his lip. Nothing serious. The rabbi was yelling, "Call the police! Call the police!" There was no need for the police. Uncle Moritz, his two sons, and some men from the congregation, broke up the fight.

The prayers did not resume that Saturday. The Torah was returned to the Ark without being read to the end. The rabbi disappeared with his tail between his legs. He was such a coward. Our role model?

Mermelstein stopped at our house. Dr. Malmos came to attend to Mermelstein's bleeding nose.

After a couple of shots of rum and a Danish pastry that my mother served, Mermelstein was on his way home. Next Saturday, Mermelstein didn't show up in the synagogue. I don't remember seeing him again.

The rabbi never chastised the combatants. How could he? He was protecting his job!

THE KAKABULL STORIES

As a child, I don't remember anybody rubbing me the wrong way, except Novak, the school principal, Rabbi Jungreis, and The Melamed.

Sure we had little spats between us kids. Like when Zoli, my good friend, took my father to the place where we hid cigarette butts.

But principal Novak, Rabbi Jungreis, and The Melamed, the child molester teacher, that's a different story. They were supposed to be our role models: Novak, the raving anti-Semite, the cowardly rabbi, and The Melamed. What a bunch of misfits they were!

Today, 70 years later, I can vividly recall the rabbi walking to the synagogue. He had to pass our house every time he went to the synagogue, and I watched him with disgust. Always the same scene: walking hunched, close to the edge of the road, looking at the dirt, never turning his head. It looked as if he wished the earth would swallow him. What a pitiful sight!

True, those bastards, the ignoramus gentile herdsmen, always made sure to drive their pigs home from the pasture at the exact same time the rabbi went to prayers.

All those kakabull stories we were fed; always with the threats of being punished for every transgression, no matter how insignificant. The constant message of threats to instill fear in us. Fear of God. Fear of the rabbis. Fear, fear, and more fear! We were told that if we pick up a stone on the Sabbath, our hand would fall off. Or if you watched the Cohanim (the priests) bless the congregation, you will go blind. No-nos by the dozens. Everything was punishable by 25 lashes at best, and burning in hell, at worst. Unfortunately their predictions came through. A lot of Jews burned in hell, but not because they picked up a stone on the Sabbath or watched the Cohanim bless the congregation. Or even ate pork.

At some point I realized that all that religious indoctrination didn't make much sense. When nobody was around, I picked up a stone, but to make sure, with the left hand, just in case. I am right-handed. The next challenge was the blessing of the priests. I opened one eye, again, just to be sure, and then the other. Nothing happened, so I started to challenge everything I was told not to do! I didn't dare to eat pork! I wasn't going to push my luck.

The rebellion continued. I kept praying in the morning, but left out most of the prayer. One morning I woke up late and had no time to pray. I had four tests scheduled that day. I ran to school, convinced that God will punish me. I was tested only for the subjects I was prepared for, and pulled two A's. The other two tests, for which I wasn't prepared, were postponed for a week later. So God didn't punish me. World War II was raging and he must have been occupied with more important things than me missing the morning prayers. I never prayed again!

Not even in the concentration camps!

TSULENT

On Saturday, the Sabbath, (Shabbos) it was forbidden to cook. To have a nice warm meal and not transgress the Sabbath laws required a little imagination. So how do you fool God? Very simple!

In winter time, the houses were heated, so to warm up the food was easy. The law wasn't broken because the fire was set a day before and some Shabbos Goy (a gentile, hired to perform tasks that observant, religious Jews could not) came to feed the fire. But summer time there was no fire in the oven and no possibility of warming the food. Why give up a good warm meal if there is a possibility to have it, and at the same time not offend God?

The summer dish was called Tsulent. It was a dish made of beans and barley, a nice slice of beef, chicken fat, salt, pepper, and all kind of additions that were the secrets of every housewife. All this was prepared on Friday afternoon, and preferably put in an earthenware pot.

Friday was the day for baking bread for the whole week, and challah (an egg rich white bread) for the Sabbath. It didn't pay to reheat the oven for one pot. Therefore an arrangement was made with the Schonbergers to reheat their oven. And the whole Jewish community brought their pots to be baked in the Schonberger's oven.

The ritual started every Friday evening. Just before sundown, the pots were placed in the reheated oven. A wooden contraption was put over the opening and sealed with mud to be opened the next noon. On Saturday noon, the crowd gathered in the Schonberger's yard. The air was tense with anticipation.

On Saturday it is forbidden to do any physical work, so a small task like breaking the seal had to be done by a non-Jew (the Shabbos goy). Most of the time the maids were around and they did the task. But sometimes when the maids were late and the men lost their patience, the less religious men surrounded the oven and one of them kicked the seal open. To make believe that one of the maids broke the seal they started to chant. "Thank you Maria! Thank you

Maria!"

The same schtick was pulled by the same men on Saturday evening before the Maariv prayers. The same man, who kicked the seal open on the oven, took care of the lights. The scene was the same as at the breaking open of the sealed oven, but now the chant was: "Thank you John! Thank you John!" So the rabbi should think that some John came to throw the switch.

But let's go back to the Tsulent.

As soon as the pots came out of the oven, everybody opened the lids to determine the result. Everybody checked everybody's dish to judge whose Tsulent was the best.

The consensus was always the same. The winner as always was Big Katz. Not to be confused with Little Katz, who was a head shorter. The Tsulent of Big Katz had a golden brownish glow and a baked egg peeked out from the middle. Some of the Tsulents turned out to be like soup. And Tsulent is no soup! It supposed to be baked solid.

This is the way the Jews of Zdana fooled God and had a nice warm meal in the summer.

EUGENE SCHONBERGER

The Schonberger family was the poorest Jewish family in Zdana. They had eight children; three girls and five boys. Eugene was known as Shaye because all the Schonberger kids were known by their Yiddish names. Shaye was about three years older than I. When I was nine or ten, Shaye was studying in a yeshiva in Kosice. He came home every weekend. Because we younger kids were seldom taken to the city and had no idea about city life, it was easy for Shaye to impress us with all kind of tall tales about the city.

One day, he told me about a collection of all kind of exotic postage stamps that he was collecting. It was worth a fortune. So he said! If I had an interest he would sell me some of the stamps. I was impressed. The stamps were from countries I never heard of. I had a problem. I had no money. And to ask my parents, was out of the question. The temptation to collect stamps was too great to let go. I had to find a way to be able to finance the enterprise.

In our store, we had a drawer where small change was kept. Many times my mother stepped out from the store and I was left alone. I started to dip into the change. From the beginning, just small amounts; pennies. But when I realized that my parents didn't miss the money, I got more daring. Never big sums! Maybe 25 cents or half a dollar. No more. I never touched paper money. I thus accumulated a large collection of stamps. Not only the ones that I bought from Shaye, but also local Czech stamps.

In my eleventh year I started junior high in Kosice. The kids in my class were all city slickers. They were so much more sophisticated than we from the villages. Not only in academics but also in the style they lived. We village kids had a hard time to adjust. Most of the city kids had skates mounted on special shoes. Because I knew how to skate on one skate I figured that I will have no problem skating on two.

I dreamed of buying a pair of skates. As usual, I didn't think my parents would go along with the idea. It wasn't a question of money. It was that my mother was so protective and objected to anything that had to do with sports.

I thought I had an ace in my pocket: the stamp collection! I was sure that by selling the collection not only would I be able to buy a pair of skates, but I will have plenty of money left over to buy an outfit to fit the ambiance of the town skating rink.

I went to a stamp dealer and offered to sell my collection. The man looked over the collection, hesitated a little, then offered me a sum that wouldn't buy a bar of chocolate, not to speak of a pair of skates. I was devastated. I knew that I had been taken for a ride by Shaye, my friend and my original stamp dealer.

My parents never found out about me dipping into the cash register. Shaye became a very successful businessman.

Another encounter with Shaye, was circumstantial. My cousin, Ella, was an attractive little girl. Shaye began to court her. It was a kid's game. Nevertheless Shaye tried to shower her with gifts. He got hold of my brother, who was six years younger than he, and asked him to bring chocolates from the store. My little brother, Andrew, was impressed with the friendship of an older boy. With the good heart he had, he gave his share of the chocolates to Shaye.

But Ella wasn't satisfied with those morsels. She wanted more, and Shaye had no means to buy more. Shaye asked my brother to bring more. He did. In my parent's store it was seldom that somebody bought chocolate, but when a customer did come in and asked for chocolates, my parents found that much chocolate had disappeared. They suspected that I was the one dipping into the box. They started to watch us. One day they grabbed my brother with some 40 pieces in his pockets, trying to sneak out from the store. My parents never found out what went on. The kid wouldn't snitch. In the end, I was blamed. They couldn't believe that a four-year old can be such a good thief.

The next trouble I had with Shaye wasn't his fault. We had a soccer game scheduled with our rivals, the Jewish kids from Cana. Most of the time, we played barefoot. This time I felt it would be to our advantage if we played in shoes. I gave my shoes to the two younger Schonbergers: Chaim and Moshe. But Shaye was much bigger, and my shoes didn't fit him. I got a pair of shoes from my father's closet and gave them to Shaye. After the game I returned the shoes to the closet. I didn't bother to clean or polish them. It was an unfortunate decision. I had taken the best shoes my father owned, but after the game they were good for nothing.

The compliments I received regarding my brains are ringing in my ears to this day. I would have preferred a good spanking.

Go figure!

MR. AND MRS. SCHWARTZ

At the entrance to our village, not far from the Hornad River, lived the Schwartz family. They were the oldest Jewish couple in Zdana. The Schwartzes had three children: two boys and a girl. The siblings were much older then our little gang, therefore we had little knowledge about their lives.

Bela, the oldest one, was a dentist, and had a practice with his partner, Novak, in Kosice. At that time in Czechoslovakia, dentists didn't need a college education. They were, what today would be considered a dental technician, but in those days they performed work that was comparable to today's DDSs.

Zoli, the other son, lived in northern Slovakia, in a town called Presov. He had some kind of business with a female partner. It was rumored that the relationship was more than merely business. More than likely, they were married. The woman wasn't Jewish. At that time an interfaith marriage was unheard of in our culture, therefore to cover up the truth, the relationship was called a business partnership. Later, it didn't help Zoli to be married to a gentile woman. In 1942 he was deported to Poland and never returned.

The daughter lived in Hungary and came to visit every summer. She always came alone. Maybe she was divorced, or maybe the husband didn't want to accompany her. It seemed to me that the daughter was well off, because she was well dressed; much better than our mothers.

We kids didn't believe that she is the daughter of the Schwartzes because it was inconceivable to us that two such homely people as the Schwartz couple could produce such a pretty daughter. My friend Zoli doesn't remember her. But I do! She had great boobs! The house the Schwartz couple lived in looked dilapidated from the outside. It was hard to establish the real condition of the house because it was overgrown by grape vines that covered the entire house and climbed onto the roof. The garden was also overgrown by weeds. They were too old to tend it and probably had no financial means to hire somebody to do the work.

We kids considered them spooky. The reason might have been that Mr. Schwartz walked with a cane and limped badly. Spooky or not, the temptation to have freshly cut grapes from the vines, overcame our fears. There was no reason to be spooked. The Schwartzes were very gracious to us kids. They knew why we came by to say hello. They knew what a bunch of little bastards we were. Nevertheless they always treated us with fresh cut grapes. But for us, what they gave us wasn't enough, we had to swipe more. After all, we weren't saints!

As I mentioned before, Bela Schwartz practiced dentistry in Kosice with his partner, Novak. It was believed that Bela Schwartz and Mr. Novak had a very successful practice. I won't go into the details. Mr. Novak ended up with a bullet in his head or his heart. It doesn't really matter which. Mr. Novak was dead. It was alleged that Mr. Schwartz fired the gun. The congregation in Zdana was in disbelief. A Jewish boy! Impossible!

The trial was held in Kosice. Character witnesses like Lajos Berkovics and others did not help. Bela Schwartz was sentenced to life imprisonment.

In 1938, the Hungarian army occupied Kosice. In the commotion of changing administrations, there was a jailbreak. A lot of prisoners disappeared, including Bela Schwartz. The Hungarian authorities were caught by surprise. By the time they reacted, a lot of the escaped prisoners were never to be found. Bela Schwartz was one of them. It was on a Friday evening, when every member of the congregation was in the synagogue. Nobody heard the news of the jailbreak. We had no radios. Detectives from Kosice came to the synagogue and picked up Mr. Schwartz for questioning. They turned the Schwartz household upside down looking for Bela. But Bela was nowhere to be found. Eventually the police gave up and stopped bothering the Schwartzes.

The Schwartzes knew that Bela survived. Maybe they didn't know where he was, but they knew for sure that he was alive. They sat Shivah (the seven days of mourning) to create the aura that their son perished. Mr. Schwartz said Kadish (the prayer for the dead) for a whole year.

Nobody in Zdana believed what Mr. Schwartz tried to make

us believe. People were certain that Bela survived.

The saga of Bela Schwartz came to an end!

THE ELEMENTARY SCHOOL

In pre World War II Czechoslovakia, it was mandatory for every child to attend school until the age of 14. The elementary school in Zdana had only two rooms. To manage eight classes in the same day required a genius.

The eight classes were divided into four groups. The first grade attended school in the morning from eight until noon. In the afternoon, the second and third grades occupied the same classroom. The fourth and fifth grades had the same arrangement. And the sixth, seventh, and eighth grades attended the same class. The first grade teacher was Mr. Novak. A raving anti-Semite.

The first thing we learned was the national anthem. Because Czechoslovakia had more than one state, we had to learn two anthems. One was the Czech "Kde Domov Muj" and the other was the Slovak "Nad Tatrou Sa Blyska."

Lucky for me, the other two states, Moravia and Podkarpathia didn't insist on their own anthems. Singing all the anthems could have taken half the day. As soon as we started to sing, Mr. Novak told me to hum and not sing. I interpreted the remark as anti-Semitic, rather than critical. But I have to admit that Mr. Novak was right. I had no voice. That doesn't mean Mr. Novak wasn't an anti-Semite. He would needle me whenever an opportunity existed. Mostly in a very subtle way. He would send messages to my father objecting to the fact that my father subscribed to Hungarian newspapers, or complimented me on my knowledge in math, but added that Jews are good in math because they are money lenders.

I had to swallow all this, even before I was seven years old. It is difficult to understand how a man with a high education can take out his frustrations on a six year old.

On the other hand, he did me a big favor. My immune system, that he helped develop so early, came to good use later in my life when I had to withstand the Nazi and Fascist onslaught. And the concentration camps.

28

It seemed that fate decided I was sufficiently immunized against those deadly bugs: the Nazis and Fascists. Because, during the next four years, I had two, nice, lady teachers. The younger one was very pretty. The older, I considered nice because she always stopped in front of our house on her way home to chat with my father or mother, and not necessarily about my progress in school. Not that my life in the school was as juicy as peaches!

In Czechoslovakia at that time, the government had an agreement with the local peasants to house orphans. Those orphans had to work, no matter how young. They slept in the stables with the animals. They stood out from the rest of us because they wore gray uniforms. One of those kids lived across the street from our house. His name was Janko (John or Ian.)

From the first day in school, (it might have been earlier) Janko made my life miserable. Occasionally he left me alone, but for this I had to pay a premium. He came up with all kinds of ideas or schemes, and I had to oblige him, willing or not. He bet me that I wouldn't be able to finish the bread roll I had for lunch. While eating the roll, a few crumbs fell to the floor. This was proof that I didn't finish the "whole roll." The next day I had to pay off the little Mafioso!

I was ashamed to tell my mother, so the next day I went hungry. I survived! My mother was surprised to learn about my improved appetite. I would ask her for more food to get Janko off my back.

If I wasn't ready to bet, (you can fool this Jewish kid only once), he came up with more outlandish ideas. He would catch a fly, and for half a roll he would put the fly in the middle of the roll and eat it. When no new idea came to his crazy head, or I wouldn't agree to his shenanigans, he became violent. He was smaller but much stronger. Now and then he beat me up. So I suffered!

Go Figure!

I attended elementary school in Zdana for five years. I was eligible to start junior high after four years, but my parents decided to keep me in Zdana for one more year. I don't know why.

During the four years in junior high, I grew stronger. I played varsity soccer and hockey in winter. Stronger, yes, but more important, I became more confident. I spent the summer in Zdana. One day I met Janko at the Hornad River. Without any provocation on his side, I attacked him. I was going to pay him back for all those days he made my life miserable. Lucky there were people around who separated us. I was ready to tear him apart.

NUMERUS CLAUSUS

Hitler wasn't the first one to enact state sponsored anti-Semitic laws. The Hungarians were as good at it as the Germans. In Hungary, the Jews were prevented from studying, not only in the universities, but also in high schools. The Hungarian high school system was divided into two different systems. The so-called Gymnasiums were on a much higher level. Their curriculum required study in Latin, Greek, and a choice of two more languages. All other subjects were on a much higher level than the other high schools that were divided into two four year periods.

The Gymnasium had a quota for Jews, whereas the lesser quality junior high school was available to all Jews, without restriction. The problem was that after finishing four years of lesser quality junior high, it was almost impossible for Jewish students who didn't finish the first four years with at least a B+ average, to continue their education.

I didn't know if I had a chance to be accepted into a Gymnasium, but since so many Jewish kids were refused entry, my chances were, from maybe, to zero.

Having no other choice, (the surrounding villages had no high school) my parents applied to a junior high in Kosice.

As I mentioned before, Kosice was six miles from our village. The only way to reach the school was to walk for a mile to catch the train, and then a streetcar. To ease up on my daily routine, my mother made an arrangement with her sister, Lenka, who lived in Kosice. Her husband, Ignatz Katz, had a small carpet store on Main Street. He hardly eked out a living. They lived in a one bedroom apartment with two children: Aliska, who was two years my junior, was a stunning Jewish beauty with dark, curly hair, and charcoal black eyes. Her brother was a good looking little boy, named Gabriel. What else?

The small apartment wasn't the only problem I had to face. The kids in my class were a bunch of city slickers. They were a sophisticated bunch. They read books, went to theaters, operas, movies, and God knows what else. The only expertise I had was with manure.

To add to all the calamities, the Jewish kids were divided into two separate classes. The orthodox Jewish kids were paired up with the Roman Catholics. The Neolog Jewish kids (more assimilated) were sent to class with the Protestants, who were also a minority and markedly less anti-Semitic. I could have claimed that I am a Neolog, but at this point in my life I didn't have the savvy to pull off such a stunt.

I had a difficult time doing my home work. I had to wait until after supper, and then share the space in the kitchen with Lenka and Aliska. I suppose my aunt wasn't too happy with the situation. Her husband had a hard time in the business. With all the restrictions for Jewish businessmen; the uncertainty of the time must have driven her half crazy. The small amount paid by my parents, for my upkeep, kept her financially afloat. Aunt Lenka, who had a big mouth, had no choice now but to keep it shut.

A disaster loomed. The question wasn't if, it was when the bubble had to burst.

It did!

My report card at the end of the semester was nothing to rave about. We were marked with the letters A, B, C, and D was the failing mark. My report card showed one A in math, the rest were Bs and two Cs. Not a complete disaster in my eyes but one in my father's eyes.

It was decided that I will live at home and study under my father's supervision and travel to the school every day, the same way the rest of the high school kids from our village had to do. Thank you very much! I wasn't looking forward to getting up at 5:30 in the morning and arriving home at 4:30 in the afternoon, walking to the train in the morning, taking the train to Kosice, then the street car to the school. I arrived at school between 7:30 and 8 a.m. I was ready to sleep. I was only 11 years old.

So much for free will!

The second semester report card didn't improve that much. I received A's in math and Gym, C in my favorite subject: history. The rest were B's.

Mazal Tov!

I got the third degree. At the time, my good friend, Zoli, was in my class. He was a year younger, a much better student, and probably much smarter. And he had a report card to prove it. My father is a college educated man. Zoli's father is a butcher. It turned out to be a double whammy. Not enough to have a bad report card, but to be outranked by the butcher's kid? What a shande (shame)!

I tried to explain to my parents that I excelled in sports and that I might be chosen to play junior varsity soccer, and maybe hockey, too. It didn't fly.

In my sophomore year I still traveled to school. Not to be bored, two fellow traveling raving anti-Semitic kids made my ride hellish. The student ticket holders had to travel in an assigned car. There was no way to avoid the bullies. They wouldn't let me sit down, even if there were empty seats. They would purposely bump into me, hard enough to leave a dark mark. The mocking and the insults never stopped.

To my good luck, a kid from our village, who also attended our school, fell in love with my cousin, Ella. He was a Protestant. His love affair automatically made him a Jew lover in the eyes and minds of the anti-Semitic bully kids. His name was Jan Curi. He was big for his age, and strong as a bull. I found a bodyguard! The bullies stopped bothering me and Jan and I became good friends.

Go figure!

BACK TO THE BIG CITY

By the time I was a junior in high school, my parents finally decided to let me live in the city. But I had to promise that I will study to the best of my ability.

So I did!

It wasn't an empty promise. I decided to surprise my parents and bring home a perfect report card or close to it, at the next reporting time. I wanted to prove to my parents and to myself that I am no dummy.

To go back to my aunt Lenka was out of the question, even though, at the time, her husband was in a forced labor camp and there was space in the apartment. My parents found a place with an older couple with a divorced daughter. The man taught me Hebrew and the daughter, who was well educated, helped me with my Hungarian studies.

So far so good!

In all Hungarian schools, the boys in the junior classes had to enlist for military training. We met twice a week, two hours each session. They called us Levente. I haven't got a clue as to what the word means. We had to change our school caps to green military ones, but otherwise, we wore civilian clothes. From the beginning, we learned how to march; turn left or right, salutes, and so on. Later we exercised with wooden rifles, identical to military issue.

For us Jewish kids, this routine was suddenly interrupted. The order to separate the Jewish kids from the Gentiles came from the higher ups, probably from the Ministry of Education. We continued to attend the Para-military meetings but were ordered to remove the military caps. Instead of marching, we were taken to a soccer field to pick up the garbage after the Sunday soccer games. Another group of Jewish kids was sent to clean the toilets. To add insult to injury, we had to wear a two inch wide yellow band on our left forearm. Most of us were less than 13 years old.

What a burden to carry!

I made new friends. Laci Roth was a heavy-set kid. He was the son of a well-to-do family. In my senior year I befriended Gabi Reich, a sweet, near sighted boy. The class bullies were taunting Laci constantly. I became his bodyguard. I could be a bully if I chose too. Laci helped me with the Hungarian studies and I in turn helped him with math. On Sundays, he gave me his sister's bike, and we took long rides. Sometimes all the way to Zdana, 10 kilometers each way. If you took one name from each of the two boys you got my name: Gabi Roth.

If I were a Cabalist I would give that more serious thought.

Everything went according to my plan in school. Hungarian history presented the only problem. To memorize all those kings didn't agree with me. I anticipated an excellent report card, but a twist of fate changed it all.

Dr. Feley was our math professor. It was unusual to have such a high caliber teacher in junior high. Dr. Feley had an idea fixe: Jewish kids know their math; therefore they don't have to be constantly tested. She believed that to have Jewish boys tested through a speeded up version, twice a year, was sufficient. Just before the end of the semester, she chose a day to test us Jewish kids.

Dr Feley started the testing from the end of the alphabet. Starting with Zimmerman and ending with Altman. The test was simple. Dr. Feley asked a question. If the question was answered correctly, the student got an A. If he failed, he got a C. No Jewish kid got a failing mark in math from Dr. Feley. However, Laci Roth failed to answer the question. Because I was next on the list I got the same question that Laci had. I rattled off the answer and was sure an A in math would decorate my report card.

I anticipated an all A report card, except history. I was right, except in math I got a C. I was devastated.

Laci got an A in math. I knew that Dr. Feley mixed up our grades and Laci got my mark. I wasn't going to take her mistake lying down. I asked my father to see the professor. The day that my father came to our school, we had a math lesson. Soon after meeting with my father, Dr. Feley entered the class raving mad. Her face was redder than her hair. As soon as she reached the podium she opened into a tirade. "There is a student in this class who thinks that he deserves an A in math. I have a doctor's degree in math and I don't deserve an A," was her opening statement.

I was the only one in the class who knew what the speech was all about. My knees shook. I felt faint. As if from a dream, I saw Roth Gabor (me) step up to the blackboard. I don't remember how I stumbled all the way to the blackboard. There I was, standing in front of the class, humiliated. The varsity soccer player is a sissy must be what the class was thinking. I was ready to take a failing mark, just let me sit down.

Fat chance Gabriel! You cooked the soup and now you are going to eat it. That was the thought that entered my mind. Dr. Feley started to bombard me with questions. To my utter surprise, my head was clear, and the adrenaline was working overtime. I answered every question. No mistakes. The bell rang and I was sure I was off the hook.

Not so fast Gabriel!

Dr. Feley ignored the bell, and continued with questions. With the bell ringing and me relaxing, I made an error. "There," she said, "is the A student?" and added some additional compliments. Only then did she leave the class.

I was doomed!

About a month after that tragic-comic episode, Dr. Feley entered the classroom in an agitated mood. She called the first student to the blackboard to recapture the material we learned the lesson before. The kid looked at the blackboard and turned his head to the class, as if to ask for some hints from the floor, and then back to the blackboard, hoping that by some miracle the answer will appear there.

No such luck!

He got a failing mark. She called the next student, then the next, and an additional ten students. No answers! She failed every one. Then, even angrier than before, she turned to the class and asked, "Who can solve the problem?"

Quiet!

No volunteers! I was sure Zimmerman would get up. He didn't. I was sure I knew how to solve the problem but I was scared out of my wits. Slowly I lifted my hand, about halfway. Dr. Feley looked at me. She hesitated for a moment, than asked me to come to the blackboard.

I started to work feverishly. Soon the whole blackboard was

36

filled with calculations. She looked, and looked, then told me to erase everything and start from the beginning. "Explain to the dummies what you just did." I did it again. After I finished, she handed me her pencil and told me to enter a mark in the yearbook. I wrote a large A. Even though I had no doctor's degree in math.

At the end of the year I wasn't tested. I finished the year with straight A's and a B in history. This was the best report card I ever had. Before or after.

Unfortunately, I couldn't share my happiness with my father. He was in a forced labor camp, and we had no visitation rights. Later, he was shipped to the Russian front. In January 1943, we got a postcard from the Hungarian military saying that my father was missing in action. The truth was never told. A soldier who served in the Hungarian army came home on leave and told us that he met my father in a hospital, near Stalingrad. His hands and legs were frost bitten.

After the end of the war, we heard all kinds of horror stories. We were told that at the big retreat from Stalingrad, the German army rounded up all the forced laborers; in this case the Jews, locked them in a barn, put the barn on fire, and machine gunned all who tried to escape. We had no way to verify the story. Maybe my father lucked out and died in the hospital.

THE SOCCER GAME

The 1942-1943 school year was a memorable one. My little brother, Andrew, entered junior high and joined me to live at the old couple's apartment. Not too much changed except that I now had a partner in my bed. Andrew was a sweet little boy. He had blond hair and blue eyes. However his nose disqualified him for being taken for an Aryan. His nose had a little hook, nothing that a good plastic surgeon would have any trouble altering.

By then, my father was believed dead. Without being asked, I took over his role and cared for my brother's well being. I visited his class the first day of the semester to introduce myself to his classmates as a senior and as his brother. I did not have to add another word. It was understood that they were to keep their hands off my brother, or else.

Andrew was fearless. He was ready to participate in every stunt possible. He gave me many sleepless nights. I hardly saw him. He spent most of the time in the company of his new friends. He had very little trouble adjusting from village to city life. He only needed my help in art work.

In my senior year in junior high, all the Jewish kids were transferred to a new school. The classes were all Jewish. Were those anti-Semite politicians afraid we would infect their children with our Jewish intellect? Never mind.

We were happy just the same!

Mr. Legrady, the German language professor, was the only teacher who had some biting anti-Semitic remarks. The other teachers didn't appear to condone his behavior. At least I don't remember any needling from them in this respect. Most of the anti-Semitism came from the higher ups.

Soccer was my main hobby. A visit to my friend Langdorf's house added an additional one. Langdorf grew silkworms. When I learned that silkworms feed only on the leaves of the mulberry tree, I was hooked. We had a huge mulberry tree in our backyard, so feeding the silkworm seemed an easy task.

38

Langdorf was ready to sell as many cocoons as I wanted. I didn't realize what a huge amount of mulberry leaves those little silkworms can consume. I soon ran out of mulberry leaves and the poor devils all expired. I was left with my only hobby: soccer.

Now that I proved being no dummy and able to make good grades, my impetus to excel in academics went out the window. I was content with a B average. I knew I could pull an A in math, geography, natural sciences, art, and gym. The other subjects didn't matter. I didn't know that for a Jewish kid to continue a high-school education, he had to be a straight A student.

When the semester began, the names of the varsity team were published. I wasn't wrong. My name was on the list together with Weinberger, the red head. We were the only two Jewish kids named. The soccer field of the local national team was at the rear of the school. Not only that, we had the good fortune to train in a stadium, and once in a while the members of the national team stayed after their workout and gave us a few tips.

Before the first interscholastic meet, Weinberger and I were told that because of the new anti-Jewish laws, we wouldn't be able to participate in the games. The high school principal was also coach of the team. Even though he was an anti-Semite, he was ready to close his eyes and let us play. The two of us were far better players than the ones he had in reserve. Although he couldn't find a surgeon to replace the foreskins we had lost a long time ago, he was afraid to violate the new laws, and finally decided to put us two Jews on the second team that had no interscholastic games scheduled.

My day that will live in infamy (excuse me for using President Roosevelt's famous quote) happened the day the first and second team had a workout. The first team had a scheduled game over the weekend and this was their last practice.

The principal, Vitez (hero) Nagymarosi Bela was also the umpire. We played the regulation 30 minutes. None of the teams scored. The second half was nearing the end and still no score. The principal, also coach, and also the umpire, got very upset with the first team. To spite them, and probably wanting to humiliate them, he called a free kick against the first team. I was in cloud nine. To be kicked off the first team and now to be able to win a match was beyond my wildest dreams. To choose the kicker was simple. Weinberger and I were supposed to be on the first team; therefore the only question was who will get the honor to free kick.

Weinberger had a stronger kick but I was able to kick with my right or left foot, therefore it was decided that I will kick the penalty. I was supposed to kick with my left foot, but in the excitement I kicked the ball with my right foot, into the goalie's belly. There was no score. The game ended in a tie. The coach got angry because I crossed his intentions. Even though it was unintentional, he slapped me in the face in front of both teams. It was not unusual to be slapped in Hungarian schools, but to be humiliated in front of 30 or more classmates was something I wasn't going to take.

I turned around and cursed Vitez Nagymarosi Bela; principal, coach, and umpire, with the juiciest curse in the Hungarian language. The free translation would sound something like: fuck your mother, the old whore.

As soon as the words left my lips, I knew I made a terrible mistake. The headmaster didn't say a word. He must have been shocked more than I. And I was sure that as soon as we returned from the soccer field I would be called to his office and handed my walking papers. Students were dismissed for much lesser offenses.

Nothing happened!

A week later we had our usual workout. He let me play and never mentioned the incident. It didn't enter my mind to apologize. I wasn't too smart. My hope was that the whole incident would be forgotten.

The last day of the school year we were handed our report cards. I am surprised that I didn't drop dead on the spot. I got all Cs and one A in math.

I was doomed!

No school in all Hungary would give me a chance for further education. That was the payoff from the principal. Embarrassed and humiliated, I had no excuse. It was my dirty mouth that brought me to the edge of the pit.

Go figure!

CABINY

From the time I was big enough not to make in my pants I spent part of the summer, and the whole vacation time, with my grandma in Cabiny, a small town close to the Polish border. Grandma's house was wedged between the Laborec River on one side and a noisy brook on the other side that ran under the windows of my bedroom. I fell asleep listening to the rumbling of the brook.

A catwalk over the river led to the small railroad station. Immediately beyond the station was the forest. After a rain the mushrooms popped out in front of your eyes. Hazelnut bushes by the hundreds, if not by the thousands, grew close to the edge of the railroad tracks.

Grandma, on my maternal side, had seven children. Adolph, the oldest, died early from tuberculosis. Harry moved to the United States in 1920 to avoid military service in the Czechoslovak army. My mother got married and moved to Zdana. Lenka, with her husband, Mr. Ignatz Katz, moved to Kosice. Joe, the adventurer, served in the Czech army as a Hussar, (horseman) then moved to Belgium, and returned home for a short while. He later immigrated to Israel, and from there to the United States, where he served in the U.S. Army in World War II for five years. He was decorated and finished as a master sergeant. Ignatz and Klary, the two youngest, lived with grandma.

Grandma was a short, religious lady who shaved her head and wore a wig. She was an in-between: not good looking and not homely, either. I didn't like her. She was too domineering. Ignatz was seldom home. He commuted to work in Koskovce, another small town, in northern Slovakia. Klary, the youngest, was in her late teens when I first stayed in grandma's house. I loved her more than anybody else. Klary was a rebel.

She did everything a Jewish girl was not supposed to do. She went to the forest, alone, to pick mushrooms. She milked the goats, swam in the river, bicycled, fished, and most impressive, was her bareback horseback riding. She took me wherever she went and taught me things nobody else would. I admired her. I loved her!

Of everything she taught me, I liked horseback riding the most.

When the other grandchildren grew older, my stay in Cabiny was cut short. However, the relationship with Klary did not change. Some years later, I told the story about the horseback riding. My mother said I had a wild imagination. But when we found some old pictures of me riding a horse, bareback, she had to change her mind.

In 1938, after the occupation of Czechoslovakia by Hungary, we did not travel anymore. Cabiny was now in Slovakia and for the Jews it was almost impossible to receive a visa. I saw Klary once more at the wedding of Ignatz to Arlene, in Presov. Klary later married and had a little girl. They both perished in Auschwitz, as did Lenka with her two children, my grandma, and my brother, Andrew. Ignatz died shortly after the liberation. He contracted typhoid, but with no medications available, he succumbed to the sickness.

FACING THE UNAVOIDABLE

With my disastrous report card in hand, I had to face my mother. I wasn't concerned about myself; my thoughts were with my mother. She was having a rough time. Her sister, with two children, moved in with us. Grandma came from Slovakia, because Ignatz feared he couldn't protect her from the Nazis. My mother was the only breadwinner. I didn't know if Ignatz could help her financially, or not.

I don't remember how I approached my mother, but I do remember that she didn't make a scene. Maybe she anticipated problems from her son, the soccer player.

Some years before, Dr. Malmos, the local doctor, had retired and lived in Budapest. He was a very good friend of our family. He delivered me to this world and was at least partially responsible for my existence.

He owed me one!

My mother wrote to good Dr. Malmos, asking for advice. He responded quickly, promising to take the matter in hand. His daughter was married to a gentleman with connections in the Jewish community. He arranged an interview in the teachers college; a Jewish school in Budapest. It was decided that I had to take a test in academics. We didn't know what to do first. So I did nothing.

My mother called a week later, and we took a train to Budapest. The next morning the good doctor Malmos, my mother, and I, went to the school for me to take the test. I was sweating bullets. The professor, who was supposed to test me, was a gentleman in his early fifties. He had a round face with a mischievous smile. I felt uneasy. It crossed my mind that the professor with the Hungarian mustache and a grin on his lips, knew that I was to be tested only because of my connection. I was sure he would give me a hard time. I was surprised that I didn't pee in my pants.

I had hardly settled in the chair, when the professor started the conversation about the last results of the soccer league. I relaxed. It was a subject with which I was perfectly at ease. The only other subject I was as well versed in was manure. I knew every player's name from the first league, all the standings, and all the scores.

"Who is your favorite player?" was his first question.

Without hesitation I said, "Planicka."

"Why him?"

I told him that from childhood, I dreamed of being a goalie. And Planicka was one of the most famous goalies in Europe. I later realized that I was too small for the position so I started to play left or right wing.

"Are you that fast?" was his reaction.

"Reasonably so." I answered.

"So, which one is your stronger side?" He continued to inquire.

When my answer was that I have a more forceful left, I saw a glimmer in his eyes. I didn't know that the professor was an enthusiast of the school's soccer team and tried to sign up as many freshmen as possible to be eligible to play.

Then he turned the conversation to academics. "Let's see if you are as knowledgeable in academics, as in soccer. What is the capitol of Finland?" was the first question. It turned out to be the last one, too.

"Helsinki." I answered, without hesitation. "Helsinki? What are you talking about? Helsinki?" I thought that he was trying to trick me. I thought for a moment, couldn't think of any other name, and stood my ground.

"Young man, you have to come to our school to sharpen your knowledge about the world. Did you ever hear the expression "Fin Vanet Biste?" ("Where are you from?") "Fin Munkach." ("From Munkach." Therefore, the capitol of the Finns is Munkach and not Helsinki." It was an old Jewish joke.

With this exchange, the academic test ended. I made it. I was going to continue with my education in spite of my lousy report card. I didn't know who was happier; the doctor, my mother, or I. I was 14 1/2 years old. To play varsity soccer in Budapest was beyond my wildest imagination.

The next day, my mother and I returned home. I was delirious. I only spoke about soccer. I dropped Planicka, the goalie. Now I dreamed of being Zsengeler or Sussa, or Dr. Sarosi from Ferencvaros. Not necessarily with a doctor degree.

It was a great summer. My mother didn't try to force me to

attend the Hebrew school. I wouldn't have gone anyway. I was through with religion.

At the end of summer, my mother and I traveled to Budapest. The next day we said good bye to each other at the railroad station. My mother cried and I had tears in my eyes.

Hey, I was only 14 1/2 years old!

THE DORMITORY

Life for me in the dormitory was just what the doctor prescribed. True, there wasn't any privacy, but at 14, who needs privacy? The section we lived in contained three rooms. The two smaller rooms were occupied by six sophomores; three in each room. The larger room was reserved for us freshmen, with six beds for six boys.

My next bed neighbor was Laci Gross. We hit it off from the first minute. Strange as it sounds, my best friend in junior-high was Laci and another friend, my father's partner's son, was Gross. I had the same combination in junior-high. My two best friends' names, one first and one last created my name: Gabi Roth.

Laci was well educated, tall, good looking, well spoken, and an excellent athlete. Wherever Laci decided to go, I was ready to join him.

The rules in the dormitory were very strict. After supper, the dining room was changed to a study. Our homework was done under supervision. By 10 p.m. it was lights out and bed time. The supervisor of the dormitory checked every bed to make sure nobody is missing. After the inspection, the exit door on the floor was locked. Laci was the first freshman to have a key for the door. He bought one from a senior. Together with Laci, we would sneak out from the dormitory to go see a show or a movie.

We had to get up in 6:30 a.m. By 7 a.m. we had to be in the dining room for the morning prayers. The doors to the dining room were locked at 7 a.m. and anybody who missed the prayers, also missed breakfast. That wasn't a big deal. We had plenty of food stashed in our lockers.

Then there were the usual pranks kids pulled on each other: taking beds apart, smearing shoe polish on the faces of kids who slept so sound they wouldn't wake up when we pulled off their pajamas.

In 1943, World War II was raging all over Europe. It was relatively quiet in Hungary, but precautions were taken in case of a

46

bombing or fire. Yellow paper bags, filled with sand, were posted on every window sill. The elevator was out of order, so we had to climb the four flights, three or four times a day. Every time I climbed the steps, I picked up a bag and let it drop. The bag exploded in a hushed thump and the sand spilled all over the window sill. Every time the authorities replaced the bags, I broke them again. I have no idea what made me break all those nice yellow bags with red tape on them. I never asked anybody to join me. I also never told anybody I was the one who broke the sand bags.

One evening, the dormitory supervisor came to the dining room and made an announcement about the sandbags. He asked the moron who broke the bags to stand up. He obviously suspected that whoever broke the bags lived on the fourth floor. He couldn't pinpoint anybody because more than 30 boys occupied the floor. There were no volunteers to admit the crime. The only who should stand up was me. I stopped breaking the bags. To be called a moron was more than I had bargained for.

THE TEACHERS COLLEGE

It was the time of my life. Unfortunately it was disrupted by the Germanic horde's occupation of Hungary.

I was supposed to be in high school for five years. It hardly lasted one. But the short time I attended the school was full of pleasant memories. I had my physical stimulations, was not overwhelmed by the academic studies, except Hebrew, which was a pain in the neck, including the professor, with a nickname of Tsuchash.

The professor of physical education was my role model. He was a very impressive man; a wrestler; an Olympian. The first day of class he didn't even enter the classroom. He stopped in the doorway, waiting until the class calmed down. It was only then that he started to talk. We were told that when he enters the room, he doesn't care what we are doing or where we are standing. He doesn't care if we are standing on his desk. The only thing he cares about is that we jump to attention when he opens the door. To emphasize his announcement he added: "One of my eyes is blind but the other sees" putting the accent on "sees." I was completely taken by the introduction.

At the first session, he announced that anybody interested in gymnastics is welcome to join the group that he will coach. Before he finished the sentence, I held my hand high. So did my new friend, Laci Gross, and four or five other boys. From the beginning, we did special exercises to build our muscles. He made us climb ropes, shadow box, sit-ups, pushups, chin-ups, and so on. After two weeks, he assigned us to specialties for which he thought we were best fit.

Besides teaching gymnastics in our school, he taught the same in the Jewish Gymnasium. He promised us that he would set up competitive meets between the two schools. The first meet was scheduled between the soccer teams. We lost badly. All the boys from the Jewish Gymnasium were 17 or 18 years old. Our club members were 14, 15, and 16. We were completely outranked. We stunk.

The next meet was boxing. I was paired with a kid who was a bit taller than I, but equally as skinny. My corner man, Laci, advised me not to go out hitting. The match was scheduled for two rounds, two minutes each. We touched gloves and went to our corners. I looked at the kid and thought: *I can take this kid easily, but Laci told me to take it easy so I am going to listen.* The kid from the Jewish Gymnasium had other instructions. As soon as I approached him he hit my forehead with a left, and I never saw the right coming. He knocked me out. My boxing career came to an abrupt end. I continued to concentrate on gymnastics; mostly the rings.

Unfortunately, the pleasant times were badly interrupted by the German occupation. I was very sorry to lose a teacher whom I so admired.

Our history professor was a veteran of World War I. He was shell shocked, and as a result, trembled all over his body. He would hold a pencil with both hands behind his back to control the tremor. It took a while until his tremor subsided, and only then would he start to lecture, pacing back and forth in front of the class. It was difficult to concentrate.

We were shocked to see a man with such a condition entering the classroom. Few of us ever saw a man with such a grotesque appearance. In a group of 50 teenagers there will always be one asshole, in this case there were 50 plus. One of the students broke out laughing. Soon the whole class was roaring with laughter. The professor did not say a word. He picked up his books and left the room. From his reaction, I assumed that it wasn't the first time he received this type of treatment.

As soon as the door closed behind him, the class turned deadly silent. A short while after the professor left, the principal of the school entered our classroom. The compliments we got were not flattering. We all wished the ground would open and swallow us. We didn't have to be told. We knew that our behavior was unforgivable.

The professor I had the interview with, the one who enabled me to continue in my education, and who by sheer accident was a soccer enthusiast, was also my geography teacher. I was very found of him. He followed my progress, not only in geography, but in all of my subjects. Occasionally, he egged me on to do better. He was a bachelor, and had his lunches in a restaurant adjacent to the school. He had a table next to the window, every time I saw him, I would stop by to say hello. Many times I found him reading a newspaper and sipping cognac. He asked me if I would like a drink. My answer was always, "Yes." his answer was always, "Grow up first." The same joke was repeated every time I approached him.

By then I knew my father was dead. The professor could easily play the father role in my life.

Ah, then there was the professor for Hungarian literature and language. I wasn't the only one in the class with a Slovak accent. I don't know why he singled me out and told me that if I want to be a teacher, I will have to learn to speak Hungarian. That wasn't the only confrontation!

We had to write an essay. We could choose any subject, no matter what. It was Christmas vacation and I had plenty of time. I decided to write something close to my heart: my village and my country. I described the Hornad River, the little brook, the rolling fields and hills, the flower gardens, the large chestnut trees, and all the bullshit I could master. I ended the essay with a patriotic tone. I described my distaste for the occupation by Hungary and ended the essay with the hope that soon the red, white and blue flag of Czechoslovakia will again be hoisted on the flagpoles of Zdana; my town. The essay spread over five pages. I read and reread the pages. I was satisfied with the writing.

After vacation, the professor read one story written by Kalman Sandor, a boy from southern Hungary. He subject was identical to mine but it didn't have the dramatic ending as mine. I was sure the next reading will be my essay and the professor will draw a comparison between the two. The professor didn't read my essay, but he asked me to see him in his office. I found him sitting behind his desk, raving mad. He told me that he read my essay and that my description of the occupation was completely false. That part of Czechoslovakia, that I described, was always Hungary, and it will always be. He called my essay a treachery. He also told me that I was very lucky to be in a Jewish school. In any other school I would have been on the street a long time ago. He told me that as a favor to me he will burn my papers, but because from a literary point of view, the paper was well written, he will mark it a C. I got a C for a well written, but treacherous work!

His prophesy turned out to be false. The Germans occupied Hungary, and a year later, (1945) Czechoslovakia was reborn after the war ended.

I left the best for last.

I will now introduce the professor for song and music: Dr. Henry Stroke.

To study music was a prerequisite. The young teachers were sent to small villages to teach. They were usually the only teachers in the village. They had to teach every subject, in addition to music. The seats under our backsides hadn't warmed up when the rumor that Dr. Stroke doesn't remember names or faces, spread like wildfire. We were told that to get a good mark for singing or music, we should ask the boys that are talented to take the test in our name. Dr. Stroke won't know the difference.

Before the beginning of the year, we had to choose an instrument to study. Actually there were only two choices: piano or violin. I was such an ignorant little bastard; I figured that all the Gypsies in our village, including children, played the violin. Then why shouldn't I? My choice therefore, was the violin. Dr. Stroke asked me if I had played the violin. I shook my head. He put a violin in my hands, explaining the four strings, adjusted my hand on the bow, and instructed me to pull the bow over the strings from high to low. I did. Dr. Stroke, without hesitation, advised me to take up the piano.

Andrew Shulman was a talented boy. He sang in one of the synagogue's choirs. Andrew had a beautiful voice. One could compare it only to the famous Vienna Boys Choir. Zoli Berkovic, my friend from Zdana, was as tone deaf as I. He asked Andrew to take the test for him. Andrew obliged, being certain that Dr. Stroke wouldn't remember. He was so unusually good that Dr Stroke kept Andrew on the podium for the whole hour, singing one song after another. Berkovic was happy to get an A for singing.

At the next music lesson, Dr. Stroke hardly settled down at the piano, when he called Berkovic to join him. I looked to my right and saw Zoli turning colors. A hush went through the class. Dr. Stroke never called anybody by name. Somebody in the back of the class, trying to save the situation, called out, "Berkovic isn't present." But Dr. Stroke didn't fall for that ruse. He got up from the piano and walked to where Andrew Shulman sat.

"You," Dr. Stroke said, "You are Berkovic." pointing at Shulman.

"No." Andrew Shulman replied, "I am not. I am Shulman."

"No. You are Berkovic!"

"No. I am Shulman!"

And so it went on for a while. The class was in stitches. The only one who didn't laugh was Berkovic. Dr. Stroke compromised and had Shulman sing the entire class hour, believing that Berkovic was singing. Berkovic got an A. Shulman got an A. And everybody was happy. A lot of kids asked Shulman to sing in their name. He, however, now refused. He didn't want to push his luck.

Not so, Sandor Kalman. Sandor was a pianist and took tests for all who asked. He would glue on a mustache, comb his hair back, or let it hang into his eyes, and took test after test, changing like a chameleon, never to be apprehended. I learned the two required songs to be played on the piano. Just to be sure, I asked Sandor to take the test for me.

Sandor played. He played an A onto my report card.

One day, Kalman and Dr. Stroke played a piano piece for four hands. They were so immersed in the piece that we felt no need to be present. Slowly, slowly, one by one, we left the class and went to the men's room to smoke cigarettes. The principal saw the smoke seeping under the door of the bathroom. He opened the door. The moment that we saw him, we ran like a herd of bulls, toward the classroom. But because the classroom had French doors and they were narrow, we got stuck and fell over each other. The headmaster had a good chuckle. He must have seen that scene before.

ON THE WAY BACK HOME

On March 19, 1944, the German army entered Budapest. In the dormitory we were told that the school would be closed for the day. We were later told that the school was closed for the semester. I went to my classroom to pick up my belongings, where I met Zoli. He lived with his relatives and didn't know about the school closing. We consulted each other about the situation and came to the conclusion that there was nothing in Budapest to keep us there. We decided, on the spot, to go back home. Zoli ran to his relatives to pack, and I went to the dormitory. We agreed to meet at the railroad station. It was teeming with German soldiers. However, there were no searches or intervention from the Germans. We bought tickets and boarded the train. Zoli and I arrived at Kosice around midnight. I didn't know if my aunt was at her home, because at the time, she and her children lived with my mother, in Zdana.

Having no other alternatives, we waited to see if she came home. My aunt was surprised to see us. The news from Budapest had not yet reached the town. In the night, we heard the rumble of German tanks entering Kosice. Next morning, my aunt Lenka, Zoli, and I, took a train to Zdana. As soon as we arrived, the Jews of Zdana came running to get information about the happenings in the city. Unfortunately there was very little we could tell them.

In September 1939, at the onset of World War II, some Polish Jews had escaped from Poland. They had crossed the border to Hungary, trying to escape. They told us about the atrocities perpetrated on the Jewish population. Nobody wanted to hear. Nobody wanted to listen! I overheard my father's uncle, Chaim Roth, speak to my father, telling him that a thing like this can happen only to the Polish Jews. The Hungarian Jews are different. Soon we found out how different we really were. Rumors spread like wild fire; true and imaginary.

Aunt Lenka had fits of hysteria. My grandmother didn't show too much poise either. Only my mother kept her composure.

The adults had no time to discipline us. They didn't insist on Hebrew school or anything else. My responsibility was to keep the kids out of the house. I happily obliged.

My cousins from Slovakia: Ervin and Bandi, came to live in Zdana. Ervin and Bandi were also related to the Berkovics. We had a great time. With the addition of Ervin to our group, we kicked the soccer ball from morning till dusk.

There wasn't a male left in our family. The only survivor was Moritz. Every evening he came to our house and sat with my mother, talking. We kids were kept in the dark about what was happening.

Soon I found out what the hushed talk was all about. They were planning to escape.

THE ESCAPE ATTEMPT

The night before our attempted escape, the two women, Katka and Verona Veresova, our maids from my childhood in Zdana, came to our house and took everything movable, excluding the furniture, to hold for our hoped for return. We gave our neighbor, Vegh, the little jewelry we had. The money, some $1,000, we buried in my uncle's stable.

The night before the round up of Jews in Zdana and the neighboring villages, our family met in my uncle's house. From there we started the journey that we hoped would save us from the Nazis. My uncle's house was chosen for the meeting because it was on the outskirts of the village. We hoped not to be observed by the authorities or the locals who were ready to sell us out.

We were 13 people in the group. My grandma Rella; aunt Lenka, with two children, Aliska and Gabi; uncle Moritz; his father, Joe; his wife, Kati, and daughter Ella; Ervin and Bandi, my two cousins; my mother Anna; my brother, Andrew, and me.

It was a dark night. That was supposed to be in our favor. Uncle Moritz led the way; nobody knew the neighborhood better. He was born in the house where we started our journey. He worked all his life in the fields surrounding the village, and hauled wood from the forest in wintertime. Uncle Moritz became confused, due to all the excitement. He lost his orientation and led us all night in circles. When dawn came, we found ourselves less than a mile from where we started.

We were on the outskirts of the neighboring village, Nadost. Uncle Moritz knew the peasant who lived in a house there. He arranged with the man to keep us hidden for the day. In the evening we continued to our final destination. To my surprise I found that we were heading for the estate of the Baroness Lila Kekedi, who seemingly agreed to hide all of us.

With hindsight, I can't imagine that uncle Moritz and my mother had a clear plan, or any plan, how to get to the estate, without being caught. They probably had none. I never bothered to question my mother or uncle Moritz about that fateful night.

At the onset of darkness, we moved from the peasant's house and took the road toward the village of Keked, where the Baroness's estate was located. As soon as we entered Keked, two watchmen stopped us. Uncle Moritz tried to pay off the guys, to no avail.

Ervin and I were at the end of the column. As soon as I realized what was going on, I jumped into the ditch on the side of the road and pulled Ervin with me. We listened to the conversation between the group and the watchmen. Ervin and I heard the begging, the promising of more and more money. Nothing helped!

The group was ushered away. Ervin and I stayed in the ditch until the watchmen and our families left the scene. I had no choice but to play the hero. I told Ervin not to worry; I was a local kid and knew my way around. I came up with a plan that was as irrational as my elders' plan. I told Ervin that we are going to Slovakia. My uncle, Ignatz, lived in Slovakia. He was a privileged Jew because he was important to the economy of Slovakia. His importance was a myth. He was able to pay off some Nazis to keep him from persecution. I thought if we can reach him, he will protect us. I don't know how I came up with the stupid idea. Only a couple of months ago he sent his mother to us because he couldn't protect her anymore. I was very aware of that situation.

To reach Slovakia from where we were, we had to first cross a forest. I don't know what I had in mind. We had no food and no money. Not withstanding the absurdity of the plan, we walked toward the forest. At the edge of the forest we sat to rest. At once it dawned on me that I haven't got the slightest idea of how to cross the forest. The thought to enter the forest in the night, made me shiver.

To save face, I told Ervin that we have to change our plan. I decided to go back to the village and try to get in touch with one of the maids I was very close with. On the way back from Nadost to Zdana, we chose to walk on the main road so as not to have the same predicament my uncle Moritz encountered. We met peasants returning home, who gave us a description of the situation in the villages. The peasants told us that all the Jews from Zdana and the neighboring villages were rounded up by the Hungarian police and herded into the school building in Zdana.

I attended that school for five years and knew every little hole in the fence. I felt that I would be able to go in an out of the school building without being seen. We arrived in the village around two in the morning. I knocked on Katka's younger sister, Verona's window. She came out. Seeing us, she panicked. She told us that there was an announcement regarding the Jews. The population was told that anybody hiding a Jew will be shot. Nevertheless she hid us in the stable and ran to alert her sister. Verona came back with good news. The sisters decided to hide us.

She served us hot milk with bread before she retired to her room. Soon we were fast asleep. I had slept in a stable before. It was a first for Ervin. In the morning, Verona brought us a good peasant breakfast. She told us that for the time being we will stay in the stable until permanent arrangements can be found. Every hour she came to tell us which Jews were brought to the school.

In the afternoon we received the bad news. The police brought my entire family to the school from the neighboring village. I asked Verona to find out how many policemen guarded the prisoners. They must have been very confident that nobody will escape (they were right). They had only one guard at the gate to the school. At the onset of darkness I crawled through a hole in the fence, into the school. There were only two rooms. I had no problem finding my mother. I told her everything that happened in the last 24 hours. I asked my family to pack up and follow me. I told my mother that the maids agreed to hide us.

Nobody wanted to move. I returned to the stable to discuss the matter with Ervin. We had a choice: stay with Verona and Katka, or join the family. We decided on the latter.

A few days later, the police packed us into horse drawn carriages and drove us to the railroad station in Cana. The population of Zdana watched behind drawn drapes. Some with remorse. Some stood in the street getting pleasure from the spectacle. A few had nasty remarks.

So much for free will!

THE BRICK FACTORY

The Hungarian police had no problem with the Jews. A simple announcement ordering all Jews to pack a small amount of belongings and move to the brick factory, went without a hitch. Ten thousand Jews; men, women, children, old, young, healthy and sick, sane, insane, bright, stupid, well-to-do, poor; all seemingly blind and deaf, walking like sheep, toward the brick factory, refusing to face the music.

The brick factory was located just outside the city limits. It was an ideal place for the Germans to use. It was out of sight, fenced, and could be watched with only a few guards. The railroad tracks were connected to the main arteries, running between Hungary and Poland. As I said, an ideal place. At the time, the factory wasn't in use. We lived in the shack used for drying bricks. The shacks had only roofs. All four sides were open to the wind. We slept on the dirt floor, one on top of each other, to keep warm. We washed in the lake, but only our hands and faces. There was no place to undress, no place to change. The sanitation facilities were nonexistent.

I was 15 years old, so all the inconveniences didn't stop me from chasing girls. Next to our shack, lived a girl. The school hat that she wore was the same as my cousin Ella's. The four gold stripes on the side of the cap meant she was a senior in junior high. She had to be in the same class as my cousin. I asked Ella to introduce me. It was easy. We eyed each other for days. Her name was Hanna, a blue eyed, blonde with a freckled face. A real "goishe punem" (gentile face). We spent a lot of time together. It was a platonic love affair. We kissed only once, just before we were loaded into the cattle car. Was I stupid, or what?

I saw her once more in Auschwitz, on the other side of the electric fence. Her blonde hair was shaven, a kerchief covered her head, but she still looked cute. I wore my striped uniform. My head was also shaved. It didn't matter. We looked at each other with affection. Hanna told me that my mother was in the same barracks. I asked her to fetch my mother. I was chased from the fence and didn't

58

see my mother or Hanna again in the brick factory. Hanna and my mother survived the camps.

We didn't work in the brick factory. Once in a while the Hungarian police took us to the city to carry furniture from the abandoned Jewish apartments. I wore the only suit I had. It must have been my mother's idea to be dressed well when going to work in the city.

Returning from work, I saw kids playing soccer. I ran down the hill where the game was played. Next to the soccer field, on a small hill, were the outhouses. The excrement seeped out and covered a sizable area around the latrine. The sanitation workers covered it with lime and it dried in the hot sun. The ball was kicked toward the outhouse. To save the ball from falling into the seepage, I ran and tried to kick the ball with my back to the field. I kicked the ball with my left foot. I didn't realize how close I was to the seepage, and with my right foot, I stepped into the not so firm excrement. I slid, feet first, with my five foot frame into the shit.

I saved the ball!

My mother tried to wash the suit, with no success. I never wore it again. From then on I wore only shorts. My mother packed up the smelly suit for the trip to Poland. The men, who sorted the spoils from the trains, must have wondered if somebody was trying to send a message to the Germans.

Between my aunt's hysterics and my grandma's constant crying, my mother had to have nerves of steel. My brother and I were not too much help either. We were too young!

Just before we were shipped out to Poland, I saw my first German soldier; an officer. The officer read a speech in front of the assembled crowd, where he assured us that we have nothing to worry about. We were being resettled to a safe place where we will be living in a safe environment. The speech was short; no time could be wasted. Most of the crowd believed the German, or wanted to believe. And so, in the middle of May 1944, we were packed like sardines, into cattle cars, on our way to the unknown "safe environment."

The trip lasted three or four days. I remember only sketchy segments. I remember sitting in the middle of the car. On my left, was a window. People climbed over me to breathe some fresh air. Some tried to figure out the direction we were traveling. I don't remember who was in the same cattle car with me. My family, Zoli, and his family, Ervin and Bandi had to be in the same car, but I didn't see them; we all ended up in the same barracks.

Sometimes I believe the whole thing never happened. It seemed like a movie I saw or a book I had read. I remember the smallest details from the first day on the train and subsequent days in the camp, but the trip on the train is buried somewhere in my subconscious.

I thought about the trip a lot. I spoke to people with whom I shared the cattle car, to refresh my memory. Nothing worked. What ever I did, I drew blanks. It seemed to me that what ever happened in those four days, would forever be a secret.

Go figure!

BIRKENAU

Then the cattle car doors opened. If anybody had ever imagined hell, this was it. Eye blinding lights, dogs barking, Germans barking, even prisoners unloading the train were barking. In the background, the fires from the crematoria shot up to heaven. We did what we were told. We were defeated long before we arrived in Birkenau. The only thing we knew was to pray. And the ears of God were now closed.

I won't elaborate about how the Germans selected and segregated the prisoners. It was written and rewritten many times. I saw my mother sent to the side with the workers. So was I, with my two cousins, and two close friends.

I soon found myself in the barber shop. My hair was cut. The barber tried to cut my pubic hair but couldn't find any. After the hair cut we were ushered, more precisely, herded into the showers. The old timers spread rumors to make us believe that we will be gassed. We didn't know what to believe. It was their macabre humor.

For a moment, we thought the stories told us were true. Steam came out from the shower heads before the water did. For a short moment it was panic. People were praying, some were crying, and some stood there, resigned to the unavoidable. A sigh of relief could be heard as we realized that the showers were just that: showers.

Before we entered the showers, we had to undress and dump all our belongings on a pile. The only things we were allowed to keep were our shoes and belts. It was my first mistake. I couldn't understand how one could wear shoes without socks. I shoved the socks deep into the shoes, but another prisoner, watching, must have seen my behavior. He pulled the socks out of the shoes, dumped them on the pile, and for my transgression, slapped me in the face. My initiation to such treatment came not from a German, but from a Polish Jew. I learned fast, I wasn't hit again, for some time.

After the showers, we were paraded, naked, in front of a table, and handed a uniform with white and blue stripes; pants, jackets, and a cap. No underwear. From there we lined up, five across. Naked, clutching our uniforms, we marched to the barracks. We were shoved onto shelves, twelve at a time.

On the train for three or four days, and standing half the night, not considering the tension, I was dead tired. I didn't mind the accommodation. I only wanted to sleep.

I was among the few who survived the first six hours in Birkenau, most of the people I arrived with, just a few hours before, were gone. Up the chimneys!

The next morning we were awakened by ear shattering screams.

"Aufstehen! Aufstehen!" (Get up, get up) "You lazy Hungarian bastards."

Oh my. I have a new name. Never mind "bastard," but "Hungarian bastard;" it's more than I could take. I thought I'd be called a dirty Jew, a name I was used to. I have to learn a new language. It isn't difficult. Five words or so. The most frequent heard is "schnell"(fast). Everything is "schnell."

We don't do a damn thing, so what's the big hurry?

When I saw Zoli in the striped uniform, slightly oversized, I burst out laughing. So did Zoli. Soon we found Ervin and his brother, Bandi, and Gabi Gross from Cana. We sensed that it would be advisable to stay close to each other, just in case. Occasionally we were divided, but got back together as soon as possible.

The day started with being lined up between the barracks, each containing about 1,000 prisoners. The second word in my new German dictionary: Appell! (Roll call) Appell had a special meaning. Many times we stood for hours until the last man was accounted for.

There was no love between the Polish and Hungarian Jews. The Hungarian Jews considered themselves aristocrats. They looked down on the Galicianers. (Jews from southern Poland; Galicia) The Galicianers on the other hand, looked at the Hungarians as plain Schmucks. (pricks).

Only the Nazis were biased?

The chief of the barracks was a Polish Jew, incarcerated the year before. His prison uniform was impeccable. He wore a pressed white shirt, a dark blue jacket that appeared tailored to order, blue and gray striped pants with wide stripes, an armband with the inscription Blockeltester (head of barracks) There was no question as to who was

62

in charge.

The Blockeltester liked to delegate work He asked the assembled crowd if there were any men who were officers in the Hungarian army. Six or seven schmucks lifted their hands. He made them responsible for orders. The orders were to stand, not sit down. We could step out from the line, only by permission. We couldn't sit. It was hot and we were thirsty and hungry. Many of us sat down in the dirt. Mr. Hotshot returned. What he saw wasn't to his liking. He was going to teach the Hungarian schmucks how to keep order. He had the Hungarian schmuck officers lower their pants and his helpers dished out five lashes on their bare bottoms.

Lesson number one: do not volunteer, whatever happens.

A couple of days later, the lineup went according to the alphabet; starting with A and so forth. Our names were changed to numbers. We were tattooed! I got the number A-10490. Ervin got A-10491, and Bandi got A-10492. There was no need for names anymore!

Hey, what's your number? It's a good title for a song.

We were in Birkenau about two weeks, hanging out between the two barracks, baking our bodies in the hot sun. One time, Mr. Hotshot came running. He had us all line up and stand at attention. A German officer came to look for volunteers to work on a farm.

He asked for 300 workers, preferably farmers. Was he joking? There weren't 300 Jewish farmers in all of Hungary. After we saw what happened to the Hungarian officers; the volunteers, we decided that we would never volunteer. The opportunity to get out from this hell hole was too tempting. I was very hungry. I couldn't eat the food they served. Every time I touched it, I was ready to puke. I was born on a farm. I knew that even the poorest farmer had enough black bread. That's all I was dreaming of: a piece of black bread. I turned around and signaled to the boys.

"Let's go!" So we did.

We volunteered together with the rest of the Jewish farmers. At this point we were separated from the rest. We were lined up, five abreast. The Blockeltester that I like to call Mr. Hotshot, did the counting, then his helpers did the same, then the German did it. After all agreed that 300 men were present, we were marched to the gate. Here the counting began again by the SS men guarding the entrance to the camp. Here again, some five SS men had to agree to the presence of 300 prisoners. Papers were signed. Only then were the gates opened and we were ordered to proceed. As soon as we stepped out from the gate, we were stopped by a contingent of SS men. They counted us again, and again.

Then the command sounded. Forward march; left, right, left, right. Hell, are we in a boot camp? Marching for a mile or so, we arrived at a gate. The gate had an inscription visible to all.

ARBEIT MACHT FREI! (Work Liberates)

In reality, the inscription meant nothing. It didn't say when, how, or if at all, we will be liberated. An attorney had to come up with such a brilliant line, just in case we should sue the SS for misleading information. What a cruel joke. Auschwitz here we come.

So much for free will!

THE SENTENCE

We were in the suburb of the Polish town Oswiencim, or the German name: Auschwitz. It used to be a Polish military camp. Now that the Polish army was decimated, the Germans turned the facility into a concentration camp. In short, Ka-Zet in German, or even shorter, K.Z.

Red brick buildings were lined up in rows, just as you would anticipate in a military camp. If I had been the commander of this infamous camp I would have named it Adolf's Heaven. I would have named the streets according to the ranks of the Nazi hierarchy. Starting with Luft-Marshal Herman Goering, Heinrich Himmler, Dr. Josef Goebels, Rheinhard Heidrich, Adolf Eichmann, and maybe some lesser known monsters who exhibited their unquestioned loyalty to the Fuhrer, like the Austrian born General Globocnik.

My name, as I mentioned before, is Gabriel Gershon Roth. My middle name, Gershon, conveniently disappeared somewhere along the lines. The Hungarians changed my name, without my consent, to Roth Gabor. The Germans also asked no permission, and changed my name to a number.

Is somebody wondering what am I doing here?

So am I.

I was sentenced to death; a slow death, an agonizing one.

I am not sure about the crime I allegedly committed. I don't remember being in court. On the other hand, I must have committed some heinous crime. People don't get sentenced to death just like that. I don't even remember the judge, the prosecutor, or the defense lawyer. How many were there in the jury box? Who were the men of the jury? Slovaks? Hungarians? Germans? Or was it mixed lot? The people who sentenced me had no jurisdiction in my part of the world. Actually they didn't know if I existed at all.

They sentenced me, regardless.

Death!

The chance to be hung was slim. To be shot: maybe. To be gassed: a possibility. To die of hunger or exhaustion: most probably.

It came about because I am a Jew. My mother and father were

Jewish. My grandma and grandpa were Jewish on both sides. I am Jewish as far back as Aaron, brother of Moses.

I thought that there must be some mitigating circumstances. My hair was lighter than Adolf's. My eyes are light green and no hook in the nose. Maybe a drunken Ukrainian raped one of my great, great-grandmothers. That would only make me a partial Jew; a Mishling. (Mixed breed).

Fat chance! There was no place to appeal. No place to hide. No place to immigrate. The gates of the world were closed.

I became the property of the Third Reich. A-10490.

THE INTRODUCTION

Compared to Birkenau, Camp Auschwitz was an upgrade. Birkenau was an extermination camp. Part of it was a transfer facility where prisoners, not eliminated at arrival, were shipped all over Poland and Germany. Auschwitz was a working camp. The gas chambers in Auschwitz were discontinued in 1943.

A philharmonic orchestra, playing marching tunes, and directed by a professional conductor, greeted our arrival in Auschwitz. As downtrodden as we were, we picked up the beat and marched like soldiers, not goose stepping Germans; maybe like Italians.

The rooms were more like wards. Bunk beds, three high, were lined up in military fashion. According to my cousin, Ervin, two prisoners occupied every bunk. For some reason, unknown to me, I had a bunk bed to myself.

As soon as we settled in, we were introduced to the management. I mean those prisoners in charge of the barracks, the ward, and the toilets. The overseers were all old timers, those imprisoned long before we arrived. Most of the overseer prisoners in charge were German criminals, Polish political undesirables, Polish and Slovak Jews. The Russian POW's were shipped out a short time after we arrived.

We were quickly introduced to the rules of behavior expected of us when in the ward. We were supposed to jump off our bunks and stand at attention every time the head of the barracks entered the room. The beds had to be made to perfection. And a hundred other nonessentials, only there to make our lives more miserable. We were advised to obey all the rules or else. The or else, for every practical purpose, was a death sentence.

The day we arrived at Auschwitz we were assigned to our new jobs. The farm we dreamed about, and the black bread, turned out to be a very different existence. The farm was an experimental facility for cross breeding horses.

The foreman, or Capo, of the working detail, named Heintz,

was a German gentile prisoner. It was rumored that he was sentenced to life imprisonment for killing his parents and his wife, or killing only his wife.

Whatever!

Heintz was reasonably young; in his late 30s or so. Tall and skinny, with a slight limp, when upset, he got red in the face and screamed in a high pitched voice that would scare a dog. To have a murderer for a foreman wasn't the best news you could get. He turned out to be a typical barking dog. He never hit or bit anybody.

Wake up call was at four in the morning. Half an hour was all the time we got to wash, dress, and make our beds. Roll call was at 4:30. One of many. The SS man in charge took over the counting. The counting went on until he was sure we were all present. We were marched to the gate where a contingent of SS guards took over and marched us to our working place, cursing all the way, because they had to get up so early in the morning.

When we arrived at the work place, the guards surrounded the stables. Only when the commanding officer blew his whistle were we allowed to go inside to our work place. At six in the morning we had an additional roll call. We stood until the German guards took positions on the outer circle. The changing of the guards was perfected to absolute precision. There was no way to escape.

The work place consisted of ten stables. Stable number one was used for storage. Numbers two, three, and four, were for the pregnant mares or mares with their newborn colts. Number five was for the stallions. All specimens were used for cross breeding. Stables six, seven, eight, nine, and ten, were for the working horses; all mares.

The whole operation was overseen by three German SS men. The commander was a petty officer named Rand or Raune. A tall, good looking man, with light blue eyes. His voice was high pitched like the voice of our Capo, the German murderer criminal. He was a Pollack of German ancestry. Second in command was Hans, a sergeant, with the same background as his superior, except he was short, and had dark hair and dark brown eyes. Hans could easily been taken for a Jew if he changed uniforms. The third SS man was a corporal; an albino. A well build bastard. He was a pure German: a Reichsdeutcher.

From the original 300 Jewish farmers that volunteered only

100 were assigned to the Auschwitz contingent, the rest left for similar farms in the neighborhood.

STEFAN AND STABLE FOUR

Cousin Ervin, his brother Bandi, and I, were assigned to stable number four. It turned out to be a very lucky draw. The foreman of stable four was a Polish political prisoner. His name was Stefan. He was a heavy set fellow with graying hair. Political prisoners' heads were not shaved. Stefan was in his early 40s, maybe a little bit older. Who knows? Stefan talked very little and always in a hushed voice.

The day we arrived at his stable, he looked us over with a grin on his face. We were five kids and five adults. The Jewish farmers! Stefan must have suspected that the bunch he was looking at were no farmers. His suspicion was well founded. Not only were we not farmers, some of us had never even been close to a horse.

Gypsy; one of us Jewish farmers, (we gave him the name because of his very dark complexion) and I were the only ones from a village. The rest were city dwellers.

Stefan was a "mensch" (gentleman.) He made no fusses! He asked no questions! He explained the chores that we will have to perform and assigned two horses to each of us.

As I mentioned before, in stable four, were the pregnant mares and mares with newborn colts. Each horse and her colt, or the mares waiting to deliver, occupied a corral where they could move freely. We were issued pitchforks, brushes, and scrubbers. This was all the equipment required to do our jobs. None of us had any idea how a horse is supposed to be cleaned.

Clean the horses! Good, but how is it done?

Stefan came to the rescue. He explained the interplay between the scrubber and the brush. First you had to use the scrubber to rough up the hide, then, brush the hide smooth. The brush was pulled gently over the scrubber to accumulate the dust.

The work in stable four wasn't as hard as in the other stables. The only chores we had were to clean the stall under the horses, feed the colts, and clean the horses. Cleaning the horses took most of the time. The corrals in the stable faced each other; five on each side. There was a space in the middle that was wide enough to bring in a wagon. First thing in the morning we cleaned the manure under the horses. We pulled the wagon, loaded with manure to the pile about a hundred yards from the stable. We didn't have to unload. This was the job of the manure specialists.

By the time we cleaned the stable and fed the horses, it was time for breakfast. In his cubicle, Stefan prepared the portions that contained a quarter kilo of bread, a tiny piece of margarine, a teaspoon of preserve, and lukewarm black stuff, called coffee. After breakfast we went back to the stable and started to clean the horses. On the side of the corrals was a channel made of red brick. The brick channel was watered down to make it shine. The dust from the scrubbers had to be emptied onto the red brick to create lines. The white-gray dust on the wet brick looked as though it had been painted with fluorescent paint. Twenty lines had to be produced from every horse, twice a day.

It sounds pretty simple. Doesn't it?

Not every horse had the same amount of dust. It's actually more like dandruff. Some have more, some have very little. I was lucky. My two horses, named Haity and Hallelujah, had twice the amount needed to produce the 20 lines. There was also a trick to empty the scrubber. If you gently knocked the scrubber on the brick, you could create two lines, instead of one, from the same amount of dust. I gave the secret to Ervin but not to anybody else. His corral was next to mine. I helped him out with a couple of lines. I might have given some to Bandi. I don't really remember. The dust that I didn't need, I sold to the old city guys, who had a hard time learning the tricks. They got no free lunch from me!

One more advantage Ervin and I had. We spoke Slovak and could converse with Stefan easily, who spoke Polish. The rest of the guys were at our mercy.

Ervin's brother, Bandi, was a very religious boy. He prayed all the time. He was a tall kid. Standing next to the horse he was supposed to clean, he could reach far above the horse. He could be seen from the entrance to the stable. Bandi prayed with his eyes closed and couldn't see when a German SS entered the stable. We begged him not to do it but to no avail. Lucky for him, he was not caught praying. Not by Stefan and not by any of our SS overseers.

In summer, the horses with the colts were taken to a pasture. In the late afternoon, when the mares with their colts returned to the stables, the chaos created was beyond description. About 30 horses with their colts arrived at the same time. Each worker had to catch his horse with the colt, and bring them to their respective corrals. The city slickers, the "Jewish farmers," couldn't tell the difference between a cow and a horse, not to speak of a mare and her colt. The stable foremen, Cygan, and I were the only ones who could pair up the colts.

The German guards looked at the circus and had a good laugh!

The encounter between the teenagers and the older guys could have ended in a disaster. The whole thing started very innocently. The bales of straw that must be hauled on our backs, from the shed, were very heavy. The only two guys in our stable who could carry such a heavy weight were Cygan and me. We brought the bales and dropped them in the middle of the stable. Cygan and I went to rest up in Stefan's cubicle. When we came back, we found all the straw was used up. Nothing was left for our horses. Mr. Roth's corral was across from mine. I looked and saw straw in his corral. Much more than the usual allotment. I asked him to remove the overflow in his corral so we can put straw under our horses. He refused. I took my pitchfork, entered his corral, and cleaned his corral, not only of the overflow, but of all the straw in it. Mr. Roth (I remember his name well because Roth was my name, too) was from Munkacs a town in Karpatorussia. What I did wasn't to his liking. A fight started. The teenagers took my side and the older ones took Mr. Roth's. We bloodied each other pretty good. Stefan heard the ruckus, came in, and divided us.

If not for Stefan, who knows what would have happened?

BREAD FOR THE HORSES

There were ten corrals in stable four. Horses occupied eight of them. Corral number nine was kept free in case a mare had to deliver. Corral number ten was designated to receive the leftover items from the trains; the trains arriving in Birkenau were emptied and cleaned of all the belongings the people carried. The food was dumped in a wagon and brought to our stable to feed the horses. The breads were mostly stale but good enough for a hungry human mouth. And the horses couldn't care less. In addition to our work, we were supposed to pick the edible bread and divide it between the stables. As we dug in the pile we found pieces of bacon, smoked beef, salami, and all kinds of dried fruit.

Stefan didn't interfere. He got his share of the find. There was enough food for everybody. Most of the guys in the stable were kosher. They ate the smoked meat but wouldn't touch the bacon and salami. Cygan, Ervin, and I, decided that under the circumstances, the bacon and the salami were also kosher. At one point we had so much food we stopped eating the soups supplied by the camp. We volunteered to carry the bread to all the stables in order to keep the secret.

We kept the meats on shelves in Stefan's cubicle. There was no need to lock up the food. Nobody dared to steal. The transports from Hungary continued to come and more food came to our stable. Around July or August, the Hungarian transports stopped. Only Polish transports came, from the ghettos. And they brought no food. Our supplies dwindled from over supply to no supply at all.

The good days were over. Again we were on the meager portions from the camp. The food in the camp didn't change; it was even more disgusting than before. But we were hungry. We ate that garbage with gusto.

The workdays were long and tedious. Men got sick. They went on sick call. Some came back. Some never returned. New people came. Some lasted more and some lasted less.

As crazy as it sounds, we survivors of the first three months were looked upon with respect. We were considered to be old timers.

We felt that we were looked upon as a special breed. We felt some strange respect, or maybe admiration, not only from the foremen, but from the Germans, who frequently guarded us.

So far, luck was on my side.

The first slap that I had received in Birkenau felt like it happened ages ago. The beatings didn't stop but were less frequent. My next encounter was when I was sent to stable number two to help with some chores. The foreman there was a young Slovak Jew. His name was Odze. Only Hell knows where he got the name, because it wasn't Jewish, nor was it Slovak. He told me to do something that I considered to be superfluous. Knowing that he's a Slovak Jew, and that I spoke his language, I wasn't afraid to refuse his command. He slapped me in the face. I turned around and said, "Odze, we shall meet again." I returned to stable number four.

After the liberation, Odze and I met in Humenne. He offered me his cheek. We shook hands.

Go figure!

THE INVESTIGATION

A long time ago I forgot about the fight we had in the stable; whatever a long time meant in Auschwitz. Probably one day, maybe two.

Whatever!

It was after breakfast one day that Stefan, the foreman, came into the stable and asked me to follow him to his cubicle. There, I met a high-ranking prisoner, waiting for me. I didn't know the man. His prison uniform was of the Auschwitz elite, with an arm band three or four inches wide on his left forearm, with the letters Lager Schreiber (Camp Accountant.) He checked my number and told me to come with him.

I don't remember anybody ever being taken from work in the middle of the day. It was very out of the ordinary.

It didn't smell good!

I had no idea why I was singled out. Neither did the Lager Schreiber. He told me that he was ordered to bring me back to the camp, but he doesn't know why. One thing I was sure of, whoever I shall meet won't offer me a high position in the ranks of the prisoners. Nor will he have a message from my mother, telling me how sorry she is that I am in a concentration camp, and she will come to pick me up. Or my father, who was just passing by with his unit, found out that I am in Auschwitz, and didn't think that it was a good place to bring up a nice Jewish teenager. Or surprise, surprise, we had a drawing for a two weeks vacation in the spa at Baden-Baden and your number came up. It is A-I0490, is it not? Let's see it, we have to make sure!

What happens if I don't want the vacation? Can I exchange it for a loaf of black bread?

Where is Baden-Baden, anyway?

The walk from the workplace to the camp took forever. It felt like a year or two, maybe. Was my hair now gray all over? I had no mirror to check. I was ushered into a building outside the camp. My escort left me with a German guard; an SS man, who took me to a small room. The room was sparsely furnished: a desk, chair, no pictures on the walls, not a drape, not a carpet. Nothing. No blood stains on the wall either. I thought, hell, it can't be anything serious!

An SS officer entered the room. I wanted to greet him with an outstretched arm, and with a resounding "Heil Hitler." I changed my mind in case he misinterpreted my good intentions. The officer had a file in his hand. He looked at me in a strange way. I was such a little, skinny kid. He must have expected a different character. He looked pleasant when he entered the room. His mood changed suddenly. He looked angry now.

"Bist du ein komunist?" (Are you a communist?) He asked. I wasn't familiar with the word communist. I answered in broken German. "Nixt fertehen." (Not understand). That's all he wanted to hear. He slapped me so hard I flew under the table. He didn't bother to wait until I got up. He left the room. No good bye. No see you later. Nothing. That's how your mother taught you to behave?

The SS guard came for me and took me to the camp. I went to the barracks to report to the Blockeltester. I was hungry and hoped to get some soup. I had no idea of what was yet to come.

The foreman came in the afternoon with some thread and a needle. He told me to take off the patch, with the number, from my jacket and pants and replace it with a new one. It was a red triangle.

I became a political prisoner.

If I could have retrieved the little piece cut off my penis, a few days after I was born, I would have been eligible to visit the prostitutes. Only kidding. The bordello in Auschwitz was out-of-bounds for Jewish prisoners, no matter how high a position they held.

I never found out who snitched on me. I wouldn't be surprised if it was Mr. Roth, the older man I had a fight with.

POTATOES

Everything comes to an end; the good and the bad. In this case, my luck turned south. I was transferred to stable number six. Calling my stint in stable four good is stretching the imagination, but in comparison with my new job and new foreman, the difference was like between heaven and hell.

The foreman's name was Yusek. He too, was a political prisoner as Stefan, from stable four. But what a difference! Yusek didn't measure up to Stefan as a human being, nor in his intellect. Yusek was a small man; bald with beady eyes, rotted teeth, a bad smell, and the gait of an old cowboy.

I could never figure out if the guy was bad, crazy, or simply a raving anti-Semite. He would kick his workers indiscriminately. So much so that some ended up in the hospital, never to return to work. Yusek was always in a bad mood. Who wasn't? Always yelling, always kicking. There was no way to satisfy the bastard.

The work in stable six was much more exhausting. The routine was different from stable four. For one thing, there wasn't any bacon, smoked meats, or salami. We lived on rations that hardly could sustain a man resting, not to mention working 18 to 20 hours a day.

To survive, we had to find some supplement. Occasionally the horses were fed potatoes. Not if we could help it! The potatoes not only increased our calorie intake, but also turned into an exchangeable commodity. One co-worker came up with the idea to smuggle potatoes into the camp, then sell them for cigarettes. The cigarettes later could be exchanged for bread or any other edible item.

To smuggle potatoes into the camp was easy. The problem was finding people to buy them. One had to have connections with privileged ones, like the Capo's, the Schreibers, firefighters, musicians, and so on.

My connection was a man from Kosice. His name was Kalman. Mr. Kalman was a business man in Kosice. He soon became one in Auschwitz. I used to sneak out to his barracks, deliver the potatoes, and pick up the cigarettes. This went on without an interruption.

We returned from work very late, and weren't searched. This gave us the illusion that the smuggling can go on with impunity. It must have come to the attention of the SS authorities that the market was suddenly flooded with potatoes. There had to be a limit of possibilities to steal so much from the kitchen. Therefore the suspicion fell on our group.

One evening, we were stopped at the gate. We always marched five abreast. The first two rows were the Capo and the stable masters. They never carried contraband. They got their percentage from us. As soon as we realized that a search was on, we lifted our jackets to let the potatoes drop to the ground. Searching the third and the fourth row, the SS realized they were standing in a potato field. I knew that some of us are schlepping potatoes into the camp, but had no idea that practically most of the commandos (co-workers) were a bunch of smugglers.

We panicked!

The Germans didn't seem surprised. They had fun watching us make in our pants. Such a transgression could have sent us all to the gas chambers or at best into the bunkers. The German guards let us make a left turn and step five steps forward. The sight looked like a truck dumped a load. The kitchen workers were called to pick up the find. We were allowed to return to our barracks.

Nobody slept that night. We anticipated severe punishment. To our utter surprise, the case was closed. Like nothing ever happened. Not even a reprimand.

After a week or so, again we started to haul potatoes into the camp, as if the search never happened.

Chutzpah? Dare? No, it was a question of survival.

At the same time that I was transferred to stable six, cousin Ervin met a man from his home town, Humenne, who was imprisoned early in 1942. His name was Bummy Mittleman. Bummy was in a position to help Ervin and his brother, Bandi. He had the brothers checked into the hospital. To stay in a hospital for a prolonged time was dangerous because of the selections. But Bummy had the boys checked out before the selection. After the selection was over, Ervin and Bandi returned to the hospital. That way they had an opportunity to recuperate.

Although Auschwitz was no longer an extermination camp after 1943, those prisoners whom the Germans thought no longer capable of the heavy work we were forced to do, or who spent too much time in the hospital recovering from injuries, were "selected" for immediate death.

The brothers were lucky to be transferred to stable eight, where Reiner, a Yugoslav Jew, was the foreman; the only man I knew in the camp that didn't lose his humanity. From then on, I seldom saw Ervin and Bandi until the fateful meeting in the office of the SS commandant Lt. Colonel Arthur Liebenschenkel.

Of this meeting I shall elaborate in the coming pages.

THE MASTER SERGEANT WENT BALLISTIC

The routine in stable six was very different from stable four. The early morning tasks were pretty much the same: cleaning the stable, cleaning the horses, and having breakfast.

After breakfast, we harnessed the horses and departed for the fields. The Germans had drained the swamps around Auschwitz. Our task was to plow the now virgin land now overgrown with tall weeds. It was backbreaking work, not only for us, but for the horses.

In addition to the hard work, the food was scarce. The possibility to steal was close to zero. The morning breakfast was long ago digested, when the soup, resembling dishwater, with a few potato peals floating in it, arrived.

If it arrived at all!

Sometimes the kitchen forgot to send us the soup, or the prisoner delivering the soup couldn't find us. It was called, simply, tough luck. The mares, after being separated from the colts, retained some milk. We milked the horses, and drank the milk that was watery and contained very little fat, but nevertheless gave us some nourishment. To our good luck, the horses were fed with dry sugar beets. In the morning, before we departed for work, we packed our pockets with the beets and chewed them all day, the way the baseball players chew tobacco. The sugar gave us enough nourishment to survive the day.

It made no sense to complain. Complain to whom? Yes, it was possible to complain to heaven. Did you ever try talking to a wall?

I had been in the camp about three or four hours when Odze slapped me, then a Polish Jew hit me. I knew it was only a question of time, before I got my share of a beating. This one came from nowhere. For no good reason, as far as I was concerned.

It was a normal day; whatever normal meant, under the circumstances. Four horses pulled the plow. Two of mine and two I wasn't familiar with. All four were mares. The master sergeant in charge of the enterprise came to check the progress. He was riding a stallion. I recognized the horse. Torok Gyuri, a fellow prisoner, took care of him.

I lifted my head to say hello to the horse. At that moment the stallion with his rider came very close. My four horses, all mares, jumped and turned the plow upside down. I tried to maneuver the horses into a position that would turn the plow back to the upright position. The master sergeant had a different idea. He told me to leave the horses alone and to lift the plow myself. The plow must have weighed at least two hundred pounds, maybe more. I made believe that I was trying to lift the plow, but it didn't budge. The master sergeant got off his horse, and gave it to my guard to hold. He came toward me. I was sure he came to help me. I gave him a light smile to acknowledge his kindness.

Fat chance!

As it turned out, he had no intention of helping. He creamed me over my back with his riding whip. I don't know how many times. To show his superiority, he added a couple of shots across my legs. For a premium, he kicked me in the rib cage. Not apologizing or at least asking how I felt, he mounted his stallion and rode off into the sunset.

The SS guard was a regular. He knew me well. He didn't force me to continue with the plowing. I don't remember how I got back to the stables. I am pretty sure the SS guard drove the horses. Back in the stables, the boys cleaned my horses, made the necessary 20 dust stripes on the red brick channel, and kept Yusek of my back. One of the boys helped me march back to camp. I don't remember his name. He was a tall, skinny guy from Karpatorussia. Was anybody in the camps ever described as obese?

Very funny!

The following morning I could hardly move. I had to go on sick call. To be sick in the camp was not the most desirable thing. The real danger was to be hospitalized. One never knew when a selection would occur. Sometimes three or four days turned out to be deadly, sometimes one got away with a week or two.

The doctor who examined me wore an SS uniform. When I took off my shirt, he saw the bloodied stripes on my back. He asked who beat me. I would have been crazy to tell him. I said I fell. "It must have been a big fall," was his reply.

I agreed!

He didn't send me to the hospital. He knew that the hospital is as good as a death sentence. He prescribed a rest period of a week on the block. A treatment like this was extremely unusual, but stranger things happened in the camps.

I was supposed to rest. The overseer of the ward didn't think so. I had to do his work; remake the beds, wash the floors, and clean the toilets. For all this he gave me an additional bowl of soup and a little margarine.

To challenge him made no sense.

At least I got the son-of-a-bitch off my back.

After I finished the cleaning, I had plenty of time to lie around in my bunk. In the evenings, I visited people I knew, to chat, to exchange experiences. It was an opportunity I had missed because I usually came back too late from work, when the camp was already under curfew.

The eighth day after the beating, I returned to work. I was considered some kind of a hero. Few returned to work after less severe beatings.

Once in a while we were ordered to undress and deposit our belongings, including the mattresses, for disinfecting. It was a sleepless night. After the disinfecting, the belongings were damp. That wasn't the biggest problem. We had to find who got our uniform, and who belonged to the one we got.

The only place to complain was the "saltzamt," (the salt officer), but his office was never open that early in the morning.

Having no other choice, we marched off to work.

THE EASY DAYS WERE SUNDAYS

Sunday wakeup call was six in the morning. Noontime we came back to the camp for a well deserved rest. The philharmonic played marching songs. Hundreds of prisoners were returning to the camp. They looked better now, marching to the sound of music, than just a couple of minutes ago when they dragged their aching bodies.

Sunday afternoon was the time to take care of unfinished business. We could walk around the camp, meet people, and hopefully make some useful connections. One Sunday, I met Geza Gluck and his brother. Geza was my uncle. He was married to my father's sister, Ilonka. He asked me if I saw his two sons, or if I knew of their whereabouts. I got very angry, an adult, at least 20 years older than I, asking such stupid questions.

Everybody knew what happened to small children. What was he thinking? Was he asking me to tell him that his children went up the chimneys? I hope I wasn't rude. I never saw that uncle again.

On one of these walking around occasions, I was offered a homosexual relationship. He promised me cigarettes, food, and a good time. I wasn't sure what a homosexual relationship was. I knew that our Capo had a Pipel (prostitute). The Pipels were the young, good looking kids, whom the ranking prisoners used for sexual partners.

I wasn't that hungry. I had a good chuckle.

The circus-like scene was on Sundays, around the building where the prostitutes lived. I didn't know if the prostitutes were open for business in the middle of the week. The only time I observed the scene was on Sunday afternoons. The prisoners, all gentiles, were lined up next to the building. An SS man stood next to the door, giving instructions as to who gets in and who doesn't.

Many Sundays I was too tired to stand around and listen to music. I retired to my bunk and slept. By three in the afternoon we were awakened, lined up, and counted. Without counting, nothing moved. As always, somebody was missing, found, and beaten. We were ready to kill the late comers, since the later we moved, the later we came home to our meal. All the time that the poor bastards were mistreated, we stood and waited for the sex circus to end.

Such wasting of precious time!

Sunday afternoons were spent cleaning the horses, the equipment, and the stables. That schedule changed when the SS men decided to put on a show for the Brunhildas. (SS women). The first part of the SS show was harmless. The stallions were taken to the ring to show the Brunhildas the riding and jumping skills of their hosts.

The second part of the show was more dangerous. The prisoners handling the stallions had to ride the horses bareback. They fell off, left and right. Luckily they mastered the falls and none of the riders were hurt. The third part of the show was harmful only to the handlers whose horses were checked for cleanliness. We lined up, holding their horses. The horses and handlers had to stand in a perfectly straight line. The commandant, with the SS women, would march in front of the horses, the way a general inspects the troops. The big difference: to make more of a show, the commandant wore white gloves and would reach under the mane of the horse. If he found dust, which he always did, the handler got five lashes on his bare derriere; sometimes more. It depended on how much fun the Brunhildas had or wanted.

After the parade, we returned to the stables. I don't know what happened to the guys in the other stables that were lashed, but Yusek, in stable six, to add insult to injury, would always add a couple of kicks to the guys who were unfortunate enough to be there. We cleaned the horses until the whistle blew for roll-call.

Did I say Sundays were the easy days?

Marching home, the SS guards were cursing because they had to work on Sunday. Whatever happened, an SS guard could always blame the Jews!

Can you imagine? We volunteered to spend time in concentration camps just to tease the SS guards.

By nine o'clock, we were in our bunks. Am'chaye! (A blessing)

Go figure!

84

TOROK GYURI

I don't know why the working group was called commandos. It doesn't really matter. Tier Pflager Landwirtschaft was the full name of the commandos for whom we worked.

Stable five, as I mentioned, was the stable for the stallions. The stallions were used for cross breeding. Each horse had its own corral and its own handler. In the corral, the horses moved freely. To feed the horse, the handler had to enter the corral. Because the feeding crib was opposite the entrance, the handler had to cross the corral. Before the handler could dump the food in the crib, the stupid horse often tried to bite his handler.

From the beginning, the boys in stable five weren't aware of the biting, but they soon learned that the stallions are crazy, and the only thing they understood was the whip. The handlers started to carry sticks in their pants, in case the horses got too close.

The boys made sure that no SS ever saw them hitting a horse. Hitting a horse would have been not only the end of their horseman career, but also the end of their membership in the living human race.

Tier Pflager Landwirtschaft was not only an experimental farm for cross breeding horses, it was also used for horseback riding. The stallions were the biggest assets of the commando. The SS men made sure it stayed that way. The horses were constantly trained. They were taken to the ring, held on a long rope, and made to run around in a circle, as in a circus. Prisoners stood by with towels to dry the horses after the workout. Sometimes they had one of the prisoners ride the horse bareback. Some of the boys became excellent riders. One was a schoolmate of mine. He was a year older. His name was Torok Gyuri.

In his childhood, Gyuri was a fine specimen. Everybody in school knew Gyuri. If not for his excellence in gymnastics, then for the fact that he wore shorts in the coldest days of winter, no matter how deep the temperature sunk.

He was impressive! Gyuri took his gymnastics seriously. At the early age of 13 his torso looked like the gymnasts one sees at the Olympics. Adding to his magnificent body, Gyuri was a sun freak;

sun tanned, summer or winter.

I never saw a prisoner take his shirt off at work. Nobody was crazy enough to show their emaciated body. Gyuri was different. He worked with bare chest. His bronze toned body exhibited to all.

One day, the commanding officer, our SS master sergeant, walked by and saw Gyuri. He couldn't believe his eyes. A Jew, an Adonis, fit to be an Aryan specimen!

From that day on, Gyuri became the only guy to serve the commander's stallion. There was an unwritten understanding that Gyuri will appear shirtless no matter what the circumstances.

The real show was on Sundays when the SS men brought their Brunhildas; the blonde bimbos, to entertain them. A horse drawn carriage was brought to the front of stable five. The prisoners brought out the horses scheduled for the trip. Gyuri stood by, waiting for the horses to be harnessed. Only then did he step in front of the horses, holding them, until the party settled into the carriage. On command, he would release the reins, step aside, jump to attention, whip his barrette off his head, and stand there like a statue, displaying his magnificent body.

The commanding officer would then acknowledge his greeting with a military salute.

The Brunhildas, the blonde bimbos, laughed, and the carriage went on its way.

I bet the Brunhildas were dreaming of having Gyuri in their clutches. Not withstanding that, a thought like this is a Rassenshande (violation of racial codes).

Go figure!

JUST ANOTHER DAY

Yes, it was just like any other day. We got up early, counted for the zillionth time, marched to work, cleaned the stable, cleaned the horses, and stood in line to pick up the meager rations.

Just like any other day!

The same routine: I knew that I had to plow the fields. I knew that I will look around to steal something to eat. I knew that I will come home dead tired. I didn't go to Yusek to find out the daily schedule. I knew it would be the same.

By eight in the morning, Yusek told me not to rush. My schedule was changed and he would let me know soon what my chores would be for the day. I wasn't concerned.

Just the opposite!

Sometimes we hauled vegetables from Rajsko. Sometimes the vegetables were delivered to the SS kitchen, and sometimes we delivered, mostly cabbage, to the kitchens in Birkenau. Everybody fought for this kind of job. The reason: hauling vegetables was simply an opportunity to put your hand on some additional food.

I thought I lucked out!

Yusek told me not to rush because the SS guard was eating his breakfast. I was more than happy to oblige. I harnessed my horses, Haity and Hallelujah, and lingered in the stable, waiting to be called.

I don't know why I suddenly felt uneasy? Something didn't feel kosher. I wasn't superstitious. It was a bright sunny day. The sky was blue and only a small cloud lingered over Birkenau. And the always present smell of burning flesh. A constant reminder of our sad realities. And a sad reality it was!

How many Jews were there in this world? What is our fate? Were we conditioned to go to the gas chambers like little lambs? Is this how we go to heaven, Rabbi Jungreis, through the chimneys? Weren't we promised to be a big nation? As many as the stars in the sky, or sand on the desert. I don't remember the exact quote. Whatever! It makes no difference. All those stories I was fed in the Hebrew school. All lies! All wishful thinking. The reality hit me right between the eyes.

What happened to my little brother? He was only 12. What happened to my cousins: six, eight, 10, 11 years old? My grandma, hardly 60? My aunt, less than 40?

Were we ever duped! Maybe we duped ourselves?

I slowly walked to the office to meet my SS guard. He was supposed to give me the orders for the day. He told me to harness the horses, pick up a wagon and tools to cut grass for the horses. I did what he told me, and came back to pick him up. He didn't look beastly in particular. I have nothing to be concerned about.

That's what I thought. He sat next to me, and off we went. We stopped at the canteen. He picked up cigarettes and some food, and we continued to the outer circle. The SS guard signed us out at the gate. We continued to travel a short distance and arrived at a clearing next to a small forest. We stopped. The SS man looked over the place and decided it was suitable for cutting grass. I loosened the reins of the horses and started to cut the grass. When I returned to the wagon to pick up the pitchfork, the SS guard was smoking a cigarette. I was tempted to ask for a drag but changed my mind.

The SS man turned to me, and in a nonchalant way told me, "You know, you "arschkriecher," (asshole) I was ordered to shoot you."

I heard stories like this before. It wasn't the first time. Stories were told about guards who picked up a stone, threw it, and told the prisoner to run and pick it up. As the prisoner ran, the guard shot him dead and reported that the prisoner was trying to escape. I never experienced this. But, I thought, is this it? Am I dealing with people of Goethe and Schiller? Where has the culture gone?

Where is the blindfold, the last cigarette? Was I watching the wrong movies? Then he said, "All right, why should I work? You cut the grass, and then I am going to knock you off."

I didn't beg. I didn't pray. I was thinking. What now? What can be done? Suddenly a thought popped into my head. No, no angel appeared in front of me, or behind me, or above me. Whatever!

In front of me was the forest, behind me the SS guard, and above me, the smoked filled sky. The SS man was armed with a rifle. At most he had it loaded with five bullets. It wasn't an automatic weapon. I concocted a simple plan. I will turn toward the forest to cut the grass, and when he lights a cigarette, I will dash into the forest.

The bastard must have read my mind. He told me to stick close to the wagon. Why didn't I tell him, "Go shoot. I had enough! Load your own wagon."

No, I was a nice boy, and brought up to listen. I continued to cut the grass and load the wagon. It prolonged my existence for another half an hour. It made no sense, but under the circumstances everything was senseless!

The moment of truth neared. I don't remember being scared. I had trembled more in front of my math teacher.

I was less than 16 years old!

What are my classmates doing now? Are they in class? Are they playing soccer? Are they dating girls? Are they making preparations for the final exams? Did they have breakfast? Is anybody as hungry as I am? What would they say if I appeared in my striped uniform in front of the class? Would they laugh, or have pity? Who knows? What would my nanny, Katka, say, who loved me so much, and was ready to hide me from the Nazis? What would my wise ass aunt Lenka, say, who knew everything better than everybody else?

And what would Rabbi Jungreis say? Would he stick to his anti-Zionist ideas? If to be a Zionist is a sin, to go to the gas chambers like a lamb, is a mitzvah? Dead is good? How would that poor coward explain the absence of divine intervention? You don't have to answer, Rabbi Jungreis! I know your answer. Questions like this are not allowed to be asked. What will happen if I do ask? Will I burn in Hell?

A voice brought me back to reality. It was my SS guard. He told me to harness the horses. "It's late." He said. "Let's go home." and added, "I was only kidding!"

On the way home he inquired about the whereabouts of my family. I pointed to the sky.

Just another day in Auschwitz.

Go figure!

THE BAKERY

I don't know, and can't understand, why I remember the days in Auschwitz as always being sunny. It had to rain once in a while. In my memory, the skies are always blue, with little smoke clouds lingering on the horizon.

I am not an optimist by nature.

Maybe I remember only sunny days because we weren't issued raincoats or umbrellas.

It makes sense. Doesn't it?

No, it doesn't make sense. Nothing makes sense here in this God forsaken hell.

The Russian army was marching toward Auschwitz. The Americans landed in Normandy. The German armies were in retreat all over Europe, and here in Tier Phleger Landwirtschaft, we prisoners were cross breading horses for the Third Reich.

So what makes sense?

To us a piece of bread made all the sense in the world!

Not far from the stables was a factory for baking bread. The bakery supplied the whole neighborhood. I assume that, because trucks were lined up in front of the bakery, day and night, loading the brick shaped breads.

The bakery had windows facing the main road, leading to the outskirts of the camp. The trucks were backed up to the windows. The prisoners were throwing two breads at a time into the trucks, just as bricks are thrown by masons at a building site. Like everything else, it had to be done fast. "Schnell! Schnell! Schnell!" (fast) "Los! Los!" (let's go)

Here and there a loaf or two fell out of their hands and ended up on the ground next to the trucks. Maybe the prisoners did it purposely

Who knows?

The truck drivers were SS men, or members of the Wehrmacht.

We passed the bakery every day, sometimes more than once. We used to pick up our guards at the canteen; therefore, between the stable and the canteen, we were not guarded. It only took one of us to figure out how to steal bread that was scattered on the ground around the trucks. And not be caught.

The truck drivers were hanging around or sleeping in the cabins.

I can't recall the name of the guy from our stable that succeeded in stealing the first bread. All we needed to know is that it is possible to pull off the stunt. If someone can do it, I can too; that was my first thought.

Usually we drove three or four wagons at the time. As we approached the bakery, the front two wagons slowed down. The driver of the third wagon jumped off and ran to pick up a loaf and had plenty of time to get back to his wagon. In this case, we had to divide the bread three, or sometimes, four ways. If we drove alone, the whole plan had to be changed. The wagon had to be stopped close to the bakery.

Stopping the wagon close to or in front of the bakery was dangerous. So the procedure had to be very, very fast. The driver of the wagon had to run to pick up the bread and return to the wagon in a few seconds. Dangerous or not, to try it was worth while.

One day, I was alone and realized that my opportunity arrived. I saw nobody around the truck, and a lot of loaves scattered on the ground. In no time, I had two loaves in my hands. As I was running back to my wagon I felt a kick in my derriere. I flew spread eagle, and landed on my belly. I got up as fast as I could and saw a soldier standing in front of me. Not knowing what to do, I handed him the bread. He took one and the other one he shoved in my stomach. I understood that the loaf is mine. I hid the bread under the seat and continued to drive to the canteen to pick up my guard.

I was dying to break a piece off, but I couldn't do it in front of the guard. All day I contemplated how I would divide the bread. One thing was sure. I wasn't going to share it with anybody. At first, I thought that I'd cut a lot of slices and supplement my meager diet. Then I changed my mind. I decided to eat the whole bread at once. It would have been an easy task. Then I changed my mind again, and once again.

In the evening, I broke off a large piece and ate it with the coffee, or to be more precise, with the black, lukewarm, something, that we were served as coffee.

The left over piece, I hid under the straw, in front of my horses. It looked like the safest place. My horse found the bread and ate it. In the morning, I found only crumbs. When I realized what happened, I sat down in the corner of the corral and cried.

For, the next few weeks I stole all the potatoes my horses were rationed. What I couldn't sell, I gave away.

I got even. With a horse?

DESTINY

Here is another one of those unbelievable stories from the camps. Yes, it really happened. I have two alive and kicking witnesses. It would be interesting to know exactly what happened. Who was in a position to arrange such an occurrence and who really brought it to fruition? The person that was most probably involved isn't alive and the one who is, won't talk.

A pity!

During my time there, the commander of the Auschwitz camp was Lt. Colonel Liebenschenkel. Rudolph Arthur Hoess, describes him as a sick man, drinking champagne and doing stupid things. One of the things Rudolph Hoess mentions in his book, "The Death Dealer," is that Colonel Liebenschenkel gave his word of honor as an SS officer, that there would be no more beatings and no more selections for the gas chamber. It is not my intention to describe the colonel. Not to defend him and not to judge him.

This is the drama of my cousins; Ervin and Bandi, and me.

At the time of the story, I was working at the stables. Ervin and Bandi were in the hospital. They weren't sick. Their stay in the hospital was a ruse, worked out by their parents' mentor, Bummy Mittleman.

One day, it must have been in June 1944, the prisoner Capo, second in command, came to my working place to pick me up and take me back to the camp. It was unusual to be picked up from the work place in the middle of the day. It was the second time that happened. The Capo escorting me was a Polish political prisoner.

As soon as we left the working place I started to pester him with questions. I wanted to know where he is taking me and why. He told me he doesn't know. I told him I don't believe him. It was real chutzpah to talk like this to a Capo. He told me that he is taking me to the commandant's office and that's all he knows.

That's very strange!

What do I possibly have or know that the commandant is interested in? I had plenty of time to speculate. The walk from the stables to the camp took about 20 minutes. The more I speculated, the

93

more my knees shook. We arrived at the building of the commandant. I wasn't sure if it was the Gestapo building or not. I was ushered to the hallway where an SS guard stood.

The Capo handed him a paper and left.

By then I was close to making in my pants. I was scared out of my wits. I tried to think, but couldn't! The only thing going though my head was - trouble ahead.

Big trouble!

Suddenly the door opened, and Ervin and Bandi were ushered in. A crazy thought ran through my mind. We knew about the so called medical experiments done on twins. I thought maybe they want to experiment on cousins? Ervin was standing close to me. I was able to whisper. I asked him if he knew the reason why we were brought in. There was no sense to talk to Bandi. He must have been praying.

I asked Ervin if he had any knowledge about our parents' wealth. Maybe the Gestapo is looking for gold. Ervin didn't think so. I don't know what else we talked about because after a short time the guard ushered us into the commander's office; first Bandi, then Ervin, then me. It was a small room. Across the room was a large desk with a chair. On the wall was a painting, or maybe just a picture, of Adolf Hitler. I don't remember chairs or any other furniture. I am sure there were no chairs, since we were not offered to sit down.

The Colonel entered the room. He dismissed the guard and sat behind the table. I was tempted to greet him with an outstretched arm and a nice loud "Heil Hitler." No, I wasn't that crazy! We merely took off our hats and stood at attention. He opened a file and started to question us. For a moment we were in a shock, but soon the answers were flowing.

"A-10490?"

"Jawohl (yes) Herr Commandant!"

"A-10491?"

"Jawohl Herr Commandant!"

"A-I0492?"

"Jawohl Herr Commandant!"

"Is your commando the Tier Pfleger Landwirtchaft?"

"Jawohl Herr Commandant!"

"All three of you?"

"Jawohl Herr Commandant!"

"Who is the commando overseer?"

94

"Master Sergeant Rand, Herr Commandant!"
"How is the food?"
"Very good Herr Commandant!"
"Are you being beaten at you work?"
"No, Herr Commandant!"
"How many hours do you work?"
"About eighteen hours Herr Commandant!"
"A day?"
"Jawohl Herr Commandant!"
"What is your day off?"
"There isn't any, Herr Commandant!"
"Do you work Sundays?"
"Jawohl Herr Commandant but only fourteen hours!"
"Do you like to work with horses?"
"Jawohl Herr Commandant,"
"Would you like to change commandos?"
"No, Herr Commandant!"
"Are you sure?"
"Jawohl, we are sure, Herr Commandant!"

So ended the interview with the colonel. He left the room, and the guard came in and took us back to the camp. Ervin and Bandi were taken back to the hospital, and I was taken to my barracks. I had no opportunity to speak to Ervin after the interview. I found out what really happened only when Ervin returned to the commando.

It seemed that Bummy Mittleman, with some other collaborator, were able to arrange a meeting for us with the Colonel. We were supposed to ask for a transfer to a different and easier commando. The work details were called the commandos. Why? Go figure!

At the meeting we were blindsided because the message came to us a day late. We didn't dare to ask on our own volition for a transfer.

The colonel must have been flabbergasted. Somebody asks him for a favor and he, the demigod, is ready to oblige, but the subject rejects his help. The colonel must have drunk an entire bottle of champagne to recuperate. A second interview was out of the question.

Life continued. Ervin and Bandi came back from the hospital. Both were assigned to stable eight. For Ervin and Bandi it was a lucky

95

break. The stable master was a Yugoslav Jew named Reiner. The most decent man in all of Auschwitz.

Who knows what would have happened if the interview had succeeded, and the colonel had transferred us to a different working detail.

Ervin and I survived!

Bandi wasn't as lucky. He perished in Bergen Belsen.

ALTERNATE REALITY

The message explaining that we would be called for an interview with the commander of Auschwitz, Arthur Liebenschenkel didn't arrive on time. The interview that you just read ended in a fiasco. What would have happened if we had known, and that we could be frank, to a degree, with the colonel? The answers to the colonel's questions would have been very different from the ones you just read on the previous pages.

Let's return to the point where the colonel entered the room. He sat behind his desk and started the questioning.

"Who of you is A-I0490?"

I lifted my arm and said "Ich, (I) Herr Commandant."

"Who is A-I049I?"

Erwin lifted his arm.

Turning to Bandi he said, "Then you must be A-10492." Bandi is numb. I don't know, maybe Bandi was shell-shocked, or was praying. Knowing Bandi, he must have been praying. The commander repeated the question. Bandi must have finished the prayer and answered, "Ja. (yes) Ich bin (I am) A-I0492."

"Are you attached to the commando Tier Pfleger Landwirtschaft?"

"Jawohl! Herr Commandant!"

"All three of you?"

"Jawohl! Herr Commandant!"

"Who is in charge of the detail?"

"SS Master Sergeant Rand. He is not a real German. He is Polish!"

"How is the food?"

"It stinks, Herr Commandant. Not only that the food stinks but it is so minute that even a bird would complain, Herr Commandant."

"Are you being beaten on the job?"

"Jawohl, Herr Commandant. But not too bad, only two or three times."

"Who is giving you the beating?"

"Whoever feels like it. I mean the men in charge."

"How many hours do you work daily?"

"We have no watches Herr Commandant, but a rough guess would be eighteen, Herr Commandant."

"What is your day off?"

"There isn't any Herr Commandant. Sunday we work only fourteen hours, according to our Capo. He has a watch. He is a Reichsdeutcher (German.) The rumor is he killed his wife, mother and father. He is a nice guy. He screams but doesn't beat anybody, even if they deserve it."

"Is it so?"

"Jawohl! Herr Commandant!"

"Do you like to work with the horses?"

"No, Herr Commandant!"

"Would you like to change commandos?"

"We would be delighted. Herr Commandant!"

"Do you have anything in mind?"

"Yes Herr Commandant!"

"Let's hear it."

"I, A-I0490 would like to join the fire brigade."

"Why, why would you like to be a fireman?"

"Herr Commandant, may I be frank?"

"Go ahead."

"You see Herr Commandant, I like the dark blue uniforms that the fire brigade is clad in. And the way they march! Just like soldiers! They have plenty of food, cigarettes, and they work only if there is a fire."

"This can be arranged!"

"Thank you Herr Commandant!"

"And you, A-10491?"

"I am A-10490, Herr Commandant, may I speak in the name of my cousin, from my paternal side. He is a little bit shy. A-I0491 would like to be the Capo in the SS kitchen. He is the youngest and always so hungry. The food the SS have is much better. This will enable him to grow stronger and be able more proficiently to serve the Reich."

"This too can be arranged."

"Thank you Herr Commandant!"

"So what about A-10492?"

"I wouldn't ask if it wouldn't be so very important to A-10492.

It came to his attention that there isn't any rabbinical supervision. Therefore A-10492 would like to be the Capo of the rabbinical supervisory detail. He would than attach a rabbi to every working place. You see, Herr Commandant, here and there, not that it happens often, but just in case somebody should keel over at a working place from over eating at breakfast, a rabbi should be there, on the spot, to make a prayer. I don't think that it is too much to ask. Is it Herr Commandant?"

"O.K. But the rabbis will not grow beards and no side-locks."

"I agree. Herr Commandant!"

"Are there enough rabbis in the camp to cover all the working details?"

"No problem. A-I0492 will hold a speed seminar so the rabbis will be ordained the same day."

Under no circumstances could anything you just read have happened. The whole story is a figment of my imagination!

THE HOSPITAL AND THE CZECH SURGEON

The horses I was assigned to at the beginning, in stable four, followed me into stable six. They were accustomed to me the same way I was to them. With two calm horses, I had no trouble handling them.

I don't know exactly how the incident happened. I was cleaning Hallelujah, the larger of the two horses, when suddenly the horse moved and stepped on my right toe. Probably the other horse tried to grab some hay from Hallelujah, and she suddenly moved and ended up on my toe. I couldn't get my foot loose. With the help of the boy from the neighboring corral, I finally got my foot free.

I didn't feel any pain. It was late in the evening and my thoughts were of the camp, resting in my bunk. When I took a shower that evening, I saw a little cut on my large toe. I washed the dried blood off and didn't give it a second thought.

In the morning, walking to work, I felt some discomfort. At the workplace I took my boot off and realized that the cut was inflamed. At the time I was attached to a group plowing the virgin fields around Auschwitz. The work was very hard. I had to lean with all my 80 pounds on the plow to keep it in the earthy groove.

I thought it best to rest my foot for a day. I went to Yusek, and told him about my calamity. I asked him to let me stay and work around the stable. To my utter surprise he agreed. Yusek changed the schedule and gave my horses to a replacement. I had little to do in the stable. I hoped the toe would heal.

Fat chance! It was wishful thinking.

I thought of going to the infirmary. It was late when we arrived in the camp. The infirmary was closed. I didn't want to go on sick call, therefore, next morning I went to work. I hesitated about asking Yusek for one more day of rest at the stable. I chose to plow. It wasn't a smart decision. By noon my bruised toe was painful. I took off my boots and plowed barefoot. I knew then I have no choice but to go on sick call the next morning.

100

We tried to avoid sick call like the plague. You never knew if you would be sent to the hospital and then be a victim of a selection. To be selected in a selection meant that one had to bend down and kiss his ass goodbye!

I had a pair of good boots. If I remember correctly, I got the boots from a prisoner in exchange for potatoes. Before we finished work, I spoke to one of the boys in the stable about my problems. I gave him my most valuable possession: the boots, for keepsake. I told him in case I don't return, the boots are his.

By now, my foot swelled to the size of a football. I knew I was in trouble, not any trouble, but big, big trouble. I had no choice but to go on sick call. I knew that Ervin's connection has something to do with the hospital. I couldn't find Ervin and it never entered my mind to approach Bummy Mittleman without Ervin's introduction.

I was on my own!

Next morning, I went to the infirmary with my new football sized foot. A long gash developed on my toe and turned purple, then yellowish blue. It looked horrendous. I knew earlier that I was in trouble, but seeing the swelling now and the discolored foot, I realized that the trouble is ten fold.

I thought this is it. This is the end of the road!

The SS doctor examined the injury. He asked how the injury occurred. I told him the whole megilah (story) and a couple of additional things that I made up with hope to get his sympathy. To my surprise I was sent to the hospital. It was a ward with bunk beds. I think the bunk beds were only two beds high.

Next to my bed, stood a well fed man, mounting glasses. He asked me about my condition. I told him about my toe. I asked him what his problem was. He told me that he wasn't sick, he works in the hospital. He didn't appear to be a doctor, nurse or an orderly. It didn't take a genius to figure out that the man was there by "protectia." Protectia meant to be protected by a connection. Incidentally, he was a Polish Jew.

I had a good night sleep!

Next morning, before breakfast, I was taken to the operating room. I had no idea what would happen. It looked legitimate. I was told to climb onto the operating table. A nurse, or hell knows what position he had, put a mask over my mouth and nose and told me to count backward from twenty.

This is it! I thought. I will never wake up!

As much as I can remember, I remained calm. I didn't care. I had enough!

During my time in the camp, my co-prisoners spoke Hungarian. From 1938, I had attended Hungarian schools and didn't speak Slovak for at least five years. As they say, when it comes to counting, you return to your mother tongue.

On the operating table I started to count in Slovak. "Twenty, nineteen, eighteen, seventeen." By 16, I was drowsy. I felt the scalpel cutting in to my toe. To my surprise I did wake up.

It wasn't the end!

I was hoisted into a chair and a male nurse bandaged my foot with a paper bandage.

The surgeon spoke to me in Czech. He inquired about my age, my home, my family. I thought it was a social chat between two Czechoslovaks. The surgeon was a political prisoner, probably a communist.

He asked if I would like to work in the hospital. I said yes before he finished the sentence. I knew that the work in the hospital was much easier than in the stables. For one thing there was no marching to work, no long hours, or standing in line to be counted. The food was better and sometimes plenty. The prisoners who died left food for the living. I had all this information from my cousin, Ervin. He knew the procedures in the hospital very well.

My job in the hospital was to take care of only one patient. He had just been brought into the hospital. He was an artist; a painter, seemingly a friend of the surgeon.

I don't remember the name of the surgeon. In one of the stories from the book, "Problems Unique to the Holocaust," by Harry James Cargas, he mentioned two doctors, one of them, a surgeon. I tried to get in touch with Professor Cargas. Unfortunately he had died before I could reach him. His daughter found my inquiry and tried to help me. She learned that the other doctor; Dr. Eitinger, was in Auschwitz as an assistant to the surgeon. He too was dead at the time of our inquiry. I never found out the name of the surgeon. Pity, I wanted so much to mention his name!

Let's go back to the painter, whose name I think was Petr. The surgeon tried to save him. He must have been beaten badly. I can only assume the Gestapo must have done a job on him. His nose seemed to be broken and his front teeth were missing. He could hardly move. Every turn was torture. I was supposed to feed him, wash him, and try to comfort him as much as possible.

The surgeon, who knew him from Prague, tried everything possible to save him. He brought food, and I tried to feed him. He hardly could swallow three or four spoonfuls, the remainder, I finished. The rest of the time, I was cleaning the operating room.

Resting and eating well, I soon recuperated to full strength. The surgery on my toe was a success. I couldn't bend my toe, but that's a different story.

The scariest day of my life happened while being in the hospital. A surprise visit to the ward shook up everybody. The dreaded thought of a selection became a reality.

All the files of the ward's occupants were stacked on the German officer's desk.

An orderly told me to undress and lay in bed, covered up to my eyeballs, pretending that I am deadly sick. I looked up and I saw that the Polish man received the same instructions. I couldn't understand why all of us who had connections, and were in the hospital illegally, were being singled out. Maybe it was a ruse the doctors concocted.

It was known that the Germans used psychology to avoid panic. They selected only the ones who were half able. They were told they are fit for an easy job and are taken to a place to recuperate. The idea was that the very sick were going to perish in a day or two, but the not so sick could linger for a while, and for those, the Germans had no use.

The selected got civilian pants and jackets marked with red oil paint, and blue and white stripped patches. They were handed a loaf of bread and immediately ushered to the trucks waiting outside. The whole selection lasted less than half an hour.

Except for my arrival at Birkenau, this was the first time I saw a selection. Only later, I learned that to pretend to be deadly sick was the way certain people were protected from the selections.

My job didn't change. I tended to the painter and cleaned the operating room. The surgeon visited him at least twice a day. He tried to do everything in his power to save him. I am sure the surgeon knew he was fighting a losing battle, but he wasn't going to give up. Petr died. I was sorry to see him go. The same time that Petr died, six men were brought in for surgery. All six had the same inflammation I had, except theirs was on the muscle just above the knee.

It was strange that all six men had an inflammation on the same spot as I. Later I learned that the six were Polish Jews and were experimented on with the sickness called Pflegmon. Soon after the operation they were taken away. Nobody ever saw them again.

I thought a lot about the circumstance of me being sent to the hospital and operated on. Maybe the doctor who did the experiments wanted to see the difference between one who got infected naturally and those who were experimented on. It is a farfetched theory, but stranger things happened in the camps.

THE DEATH OF MY PATIENT

After my patient Petr, the painter, died, the surgeon came to see me. He advised me to go back to work. He told me that he doesn't know how long he is going to stay in Auschwitz. Rumors were that the hospital staff would be moved. The surgeon was ready to arrange a working place of my choice, but I preferred to go back to the stables.

The next morning I checked out of the hospital and reported to the Capo of my commando. The room foreman was the same as before. He knew me from the time I spent a week recuperating from the beating. I asked for my bunk. He gave it to me with no argument.

To survive in the camp for a prolonged time gave you certain status. Prolonged time? Let's say three months!

Not only the foreman, but the German guards treated us differently. I dare say, with a bit of respect. Who was a "good" German guard? Was he the one who prolongs your suffering; the one that lets you die slowly or the one that sends you to the gas chambers? The difference: being sent to the gas chambers was the end of ends, whereas working and suffering left one with a glimmer of hope to survive. Therefore the guard that tortured, let us suffer, preventing us from dying instantly, became in our eyes, the "good" German.

What an irony!

Go figure!

I would like to introduce you to one of the "good" guys.

I made sure to be in the last row when marching to work. The reason: nobody marched behind me, so I wasn't stepped on by some guy who couldn't hold the step. The same SS man marched next to me. He was bored. He found a game to play with me. He talked Yiddish to me. I told him that I don't understand the language. He asked me if I am Jewish. I told him I am. So he said, "How come I am an SS and speak Yiddish and you, the Jew, doesn't?" This went on every time going to work or going home. Same questions, same answers.

He was a small guy. He had dark hair and dark eyes. He was

from Rumania, of German ancestry. I should have asked him to change places. I was taller, had light hair, and green eyes. He would have passed for a Jew easier than I, and I could have passed for a German, easier than he. To boot, he spoke Yiddish and I didn't!

This kind of interchange between an SS and a prisoner sounded very innocent. I don't know what the little Rumanian Gypsy was all about, but in my eyes he passed for a "good guy."

Yusek, in stable six, gave me a big hello. I would have preferred to be assigned to stable four or eight, where Ervin and Bandi worked under the Yugoslav foreman. I wanted to have my horses, Haity and Hallelujah, but they were in stable six.

I forgave Hallelujah for stepping on my foot. It turned out to be a lucky break. I recuperated in the hospital. I grew and was bigger and stronger than before. A lot of the guys I worked with there were gone. Nobody knew what happened to them.

They just disappeared!

New faces replaced them; mostly young, Polish kids from the ghettos. The guards also changed. They seemed to be older. They claimed to be Wehrmacht, not SS.

Who knows?

The foremen, the Capo, and the three German SS overseers were the same.

The work also changed. We hauled manure to the fields. The work was backbreaking. One man had to load the wagon and spread the manure on the fields. It took a whole day to make one run. The guards cursed because they were forced to smell manure all day. The food was scarce. Hauling manure gave us no opportunity to steal. Oh, where were the good days of bacon, smoked meat, and the occasional piece of salami?

Torok Gyuri didn't take his shirt off anymore. He got skinny and his face was drawn. Only the sparkle in his eye remained. The only kid who looked good was the Capo's Pipel (prostitute) with his round face and round derriere. I was in good shape. I recuperated in the hospital and the weariness didn't show.

Not yet!

It was October. It began to get cold. Our uniforms were the same as in the summer. The days were shorter, but the work days seemed longer. Standing in line to be counted became more irritating.

We became less tolerant of the prisoners who fell asleep, forcing us to wait until they were found. Back then we laughed about that. We found it funny to see a guy caught sleeping, squirming to avoid some slaps from one of the foreman, or anybody waiting to give him a kick. Now we got angry and were ready to kill.

Ervin and Bandi worked in stable eight. We seldom saw each other. Somehow, there was less and less free time. We became tired sooner and took more time to recuperate. There was no time for socializing. We were happy to be able to stretch out our tired bones as soon as we arrived back in our home; the barracks.

Home? Am I kidding?

I AM NOT SS, I AM WEHRMACHT

I am sure that a lot that happened in Auschwitz escaped my memory. On the other hand, some events are still very vivid, as though they occurred yesterday.

The season for fertilizing the fields came to an end. The manure pile got smaller. What's next was the question in everybody's mind. We were certain they wouldn't allow us to sit idle.

It must have been sometime in early October 1944, when I got a new job. I didn't ask for it! Did anybody ever ask whether they considered a particular job or not?

We usually worked in a group; three to four wagons at a time with one SS guard. That early October morning, I was instructed by Yusek to see a guard in the office about instructions for the day. I thought this is one of those odd jobs that pop up once in a while.

Was I ever right!

An odd job it was. The oddest I ever had to do.

I met the guard at the office. To me he looked old. The last time I saw my father he was forty-seven. This guard looked much older than that.

As soon as we crossed the checkpoint, he asked if I knew where crematorium number one was. He told me that he arrived here only yesterday. He added that he is not an SS, that he served on the Russian front in the Wehrmacht, was injured, and transferred to guard duty in Auschwitz. His uniform was given to him only the day before.

I thought: I piss on you man, Wehrmacht, Shmermacht, you are all the same! He was new and had no idea of the routines. Let me try my luck. I told him that when we are out all day working, it is his responsibility to make sure I get my soup at noon. He asked me if we bring lunch from the stables. I explained, in detail, about the daily rations we are given. He couldn't believe that we are able to survive on so little. "What do you have under the seat?" he asked. It was his side pack. I got the message, but wasn't sure how to react. "Why don't you eat now? It will take a while till noon." This was a straight invitation to pick up his bag and eat whatever food it contained. It wasn't much, but more than I had for breakfast. I didn't believe in my good luck.

This man was for real!

I got gutsy. I asked him why he is interested in the crematorium. He told me that my job is to pick up the ashes and spread them on the fields we had plowed that summer.

Holy Molley!

I knew that the only guys working in the crematorium were the so called Sonder Commandos. The rumor was that after three months of working in the crematorium they were all eliminated. To become a Sonder Commando was as good as a death warrant. My sixteenth birthday was close. Will I celebrate the seventeenth?

We arrived at the crematorium. Papers were signed and I was told to stay close to my wagon. Prisoners from the Sonder Commando came to load the wagon. The guard brought me a bowl of soup. It was four times as much as we got at the stables and much tastier to boot. The guard asked me to drive him to the German canteen. The food that he picked up there, he didn't share, but the next morning he gave me his food again. The job lasted only a short while.

It ended with a bang!

I had just finished scattering the ashes when we heard explosions and small arms fire. My guard was an experienced soldier. He immediately realized that something is not kosher. "Let's get the hell out of here" was his first reaction. Then we heard the sirens bellowing. We heard shots fired, but by that time we were a good distance from Birkenau.

The next day we heard about the revolt of the prisoners in one of the crematoriums. Unfortunately all the prisoners taking part in the revolt, and the subsequent escape, were caught and executed the same day.

My job of picking up ashes from the crematoriums was discontinued. I don't know what happened to the SS men, or old Wehrmacht man, my guard, and in a strange way, my savior, if only for a short time. Maybe he got sick from what he saw and asked for a transfer to the Russian front.

The manure hauling came to an end. Rumors were spreading that we would be transferred to a new place. This kind of news was always worrisome. We could not fathom what a new place would be like. The question was: what if we are taken to Birkenau?

Days went by. The rumors subsided but the tension remained.

A fighter plane strafed the stables. Nobody was injured. We knew then and there that our days in Auschwitz were coming to an end.

A week later we were packing!

PLAVY

We packed. Not our personal belongings. Those we were able to pack in less than ten seconds. We always traveled light! We packed the farm equipment, food for the horses, brushes, scrubbers; in a word, everything belonging to the stable. Everything was done in secret. It made no sense to keep the move a secret. There was no reason in the world to handle the move as a secret military mission. The Germans were petrified of the thought that somebody would escape and bring the horror stories to the knowledge of the outside world.

Only part of the commando was moved. The pregnant mares and stallions were left in Auschwitz. The choice of who moves and who stays must have been done randomly. The new place was Plavy. None of us ever heard of the name. The camp consisted of two barracks; one for men and one for women, divided by barbed wire. There were electric bulbs around the fence, but I don't think the fence was electrified. A huge barn stood in the middle of the encampment and two stables for the horses.

The new camp was prepared in advance. The barracks were heated with wood burning stoves. Everybody had his own bunk. It was clean, warm, and cozy.

The prisoners that arrived before us were cooking potatoes on the stoves. Nobody bothered us. Am' chaye (a blessing.)

I was in my bunk when new prisoners arrived. I saw a familiar face. It was Geza Bruder, a kid who had a grandma in my village. He used to spend summers in Zdana. I jumped off my bunk to greet him.

"What are you doing here?" I asked.

"The same as you." was his answer.

"No, I mean where are you coming from?"

He told me that he worked in a fishery.

"What is a fishery?" I asked.

"We grow fish, stupid." was his friendly answer.

We were happy to see each other.

My job was to haul excrement from camp Auschwitz, in a large tank with an opening in the top. The tank looked like the ones that deliver oil, but much smaller. There was a second tank, driven by a tall, skinny kid from Karpatorussia, I don't remember his name. He was from Munkacs or Hust. Whatever!

Together, we drove the tanks to Auschwitz, and had the same guard, without whom, we couldn't move around, except when we entered the large circle around the camp. We soon realized that the guards tried to keep away as far as possible from us. No wonder! The stink from the excrement was unbearable. Making certain that we will not be checked, we started to smuggle potatoes into the camp. Potatoes were exchanged for cigarettes. Cigarettes were the best currency. They were easy to hide. Occasionally a loaf of bread could be bought for between 10 and 20 cigarettes. A hundred cigarettes made one a millionaire, I had many more. I had the cigarettes hidden in a hole that I dug next to my horses. I hoped the horses wouldn't eat my cigarettes the way they ate my bread.

With Geza Bruder, we hatched a plan to smuggle live fish into the Auschwitz camp. Geza was supposed to bring a pail of live fish. I wanted to build a contraption that would lower the pail into the tank. I am sure if I had stayed longer in Plavy we would have had a big business going.

It was now December 1944. It was cold. The grounds were covered with snow. There was very little work. Here and there we were sent to haul straw or hay for the horses. Most of the horsemen hung out in the stables, cleaning the horses and the stable. But most of the time we went into the barracks to bake potatoes or just warm up. The discipline wasn't the same as before. We saw very little of SS in charge. We had no knowledge that the Russian Army was so close.

By January, we began to suspect that our stay in Plavy was near an end. In the middle of January we were told to pack. The wagons were loaded with straw, hay, and oat food for the horses. And all the equipment, including pitchforks and shovels. In one word: everything.

One afternoon in January, it might have been the nineteenth; the caravan from Plavy was on its way, going west. The snow was falling. It was cold. Our move coincided with the "Death March." Hundreds or maybe thousands of people were marching toward the west. The roads were jammed with prisoners. There were men and women dragging their emaciated bodies, dressed in rags, in ankle deep snow. The guards screaming, "Schnell, Schnell, Los, Los," and shooting everybody who fell behind. The side of the road was painted with fresh blood. When night fell, the red blood turned into black blotches. The bastards ran out of bullets at the war front, but had enough for the big enemy: "The International Jew"

The marchers were pushed to the side to provide space for us to pass. It was more important to save the horses!

GOING WEST

The retreat westward was very slow. Not only the Birkenau prisoners marched, the whole German army was in full retreat. Every time they passed, with their large and small trucks, and motorcycles with side boats, we had to stop and allow the military caravan to pass. We made little progress. In the evening we stopped at a small village. The SS requisitioned stables and barns for the horses. They forced the peasants to give us food for the horses but not for us prisoners. We slept with the animals. It stunk, but it was warm.

I don't think anybody ever made sense of the "Death March." Too many bullets were wasted on those emaciated prisoners, who would have perished anyway, without the help of the SS.

At the time, the Germans had conscripted children to fight the Russians and the Americans. Yet, here, on the "Death March," able bodied, young SS men were fighting "The International Jew!" What a formidable army those Germans had to face. We men and women in rags, hungry, frozen, and sick, were dragging our feet in ankle deep snow. The only understandable reason: the Germans were afraid to face the crazy Russians now driving on Berlin.

It was so much easier to shoot the Jews. The Jews didn't shoot back!

The prisoners marching from Birkenau disappeared by the third or fourth day. The caravan with the horses continued. We spent the nights in barns and stables requisitioned by our guards. Here and there, some peasant women gave us something to eat.

The horses wore cleats on their horseshoes in the winter. Every evening we had to take off the cleats and then replace them in the morning. One evening I was so tired, I had no strength to remove the cleats from my horses. I thought that maybe if I could rest for while, I could then do the job. I was awakened by a ruckus. The horses were so close to each other, they became wild and started kicking each other. One of my horses (Hallelujah) had a gash about a foot long on her hind leg. I immediately removed the cleats, to avoid being accused of dereliction of duty.

I couldn't fall asleep.

Who knew what reaction the SS commander would have? I went to see him in the morning. I told him what happened, awaiting the worst. He came to the stable, checked the horse and realized it couldn't continue. He sold my Hallelujah and the wagon to a peasant. I was left with one horse. The SS man kept that horse as a substitute in case some other horse got hurt.

I hitched a ride with a wagon filled with hay. I crawled deep into the hay so nobody could see me. The snow continued to fall and got deeper and deeper.

The caravan continued. I felt a jolt at once. I looked up and what I saw was not funny. The Polish kid drivers had driven the wagon off the road. A tree was wedged between the wagon and the wheels. The two young kids had no idea of what to do. They yanked on the horses' reins and tried to back up, but to no avail. I had to crawl out from my hideout. I harnessed the two horses to the back of the wagon and pulled it onto the road. I returned the horses to the kid drivers and crawled back into the hay. I had hardly settled down when I felt another jerk. I knew what happened. Again we pulled the wagon to the road, and having no other choice, I took over the reins. We were so immersed in freeing the wagon we didn't realize how much effort it took. It was getting dark and there wasn't a soul around. The caravan was long gone and so were the German guards. It didn't enter my mind to turn around and head in the other direction. The Russian Army was so close! I egged the horses on to speed up their steps. I was afraid that a German guard would come along and finish us off.

The two Polish kids crawled into the hay. They were happy that I took over the reins. The snow was falling hard. The tracks of the caravan were covered. It was dark and the only thing I could see was the glow of the white snow and the trees on both sides of the road. That kept me for losing my way. In the next village, we caught up with the caravan. I had to beg an SS guard to requisition a stable for our horses. The food was gone. We were very hungry. The three of us had had no food the whole day. The two Polish kids were professional beggars. They found a peasant woman who took pity on us and gave us food. At the end of the day we had a better meal than the German rations.

Next morning we continued heading west. I decided to change company. I approached one of the wagons with hay, and told the man that the commander told me to hitch my single horse to his wagon. He didn't object. He was happy to have a companion.

One evening when I was standing at the side of the road, watching the last of the caravan coming for the night's rest, I couldn't believe my eyes. It was Zoli driving a carriage with two beautiful horses. Zoli was an orderly to one of the SS commanders. He had more food than the rest of us. He didn't ask if I am hungry. He reached under the seat and threw a loaf of bred into my outstretched hands.

After the war I mentioned that occasion to Zoli. He didn't remember it. But how could I forget the scene of a loaf flying my way?

It had to be a week or so, on a clear day, when from nowhere, "Katyusha" rockets started to fly over our heads. The German guards disappeared. We were alone for maybe two to three hours. We were sure the Russian forces would liberate us. As unexpectedly as the barrage of "Katyusha" started, it abruptly stopped. The German guards returned and we continued our journey.

A couple of days later, we stopped for a whole day to rest. It was a German village. I overheard a conversation between the farmer and a guard. The farmer asked in what unit are the guys in the striped uniforms. The farmer had no idea that we were prisoners from a concentration camp. Was he a dummy or only pretending? Who knows?

In the village, we greased the wagon wheels, loaded hay, and all kind of necessities for the continuing trip. We had no idea where we were headed. We only knew that the direction was west.

My boots were long gone. I had wooden clogs. Walking around the barn, I found a pair of brand new shoes. They were of the military kind. The shoes were not my size but with the help of rags, I managed. It was stupid of me to think that a pair of shoes would be lying around for me to find.

What really happened: one of the prisoners stole a valise that belonged to one of the German guards. He ate the food and dumped the rest in the barn. Some prisoners picked up a pair of socks, some an undershirt, but I, the idiot, took the shoes. The guard caught me with the shoes and accused me of stealing his valise. I was sure he would knock me off on the spot. Instead he took me to the commanding officer that knew me well. He was the SS man who beat the shit out of me when plowing. The officer also knew that I was one of his best

116

workers. He let me go. He told the guard to search for his valise. Go figure!

A WEEK IN CZECHOSLOVAKIA

After two weeks on the road, under sub-human conditions, and freezing in our designer pajamas, with clogs to match, we arrived in Czechoslovakia, just over the western border of Poland.

It was early afternoon. We had to wait until the SS officer requisitioned stables for the horses and living quarters for the guards.

Since I was taking care of only one horse, I had to wait until the rest were settled. I was given an address of a house at the end of the village. The guard didn't bother to accompany me. The peasant had been told that somebody was coming. He had a place prepared for my horse. The peasant spoke to me in accented German. I tried my luck, and told him in Slovak, that I don't understand German.

Bingo! The man was a Czech. I told him we would have no problem communicating because I understand Czech. I felt that he wanted to start a conversation but hesitated. I didn't know how to react. I fed my horse, removed the cleats, and cleaned the animal, just in case the German guard came to check.

All I wanted to do was take off my clogs to check my toe. I felt some pain all during the caravan but my feet were frozen most of the time and the foot was numb.

The lady of the house came to the stable and asked me to join them for supper. I couldn't believe my good luck. I asked the woman for a pail of hot water to wash up. After supper I asked again for hot water to soak my feet. When I took off the clogs, I saw the toe that had been operated on was bloody. I washed off the blood and asked the lady for some old newspaper to wrap my foot. As soon as I got into my clogs I was ready to go to the stable to sleep, but the hostess told me she had prepared a corner in the kitchen for me to sleep.

Imagine, a warm clean place to sleep, instead of a stable stinking of manure? In the middle of the night I was awakened by the housewife. A man was standing next to her. The housewife motioned for me to be quiet. The man standing next to her was the village doctor. I would give away days of my life, to remember that place and the names of the people. The doctor cleaned the wound, put on some ointment, bandaged my foot, and told me that he will be back the next

118

night. I thanked him and the housewife. I motioned with my finger on my lips to let them know my lips are sealed.

The next morning, the German guard didn't show up. I had a "five star breakfast." The hostess watched me gobble up whatever she put in front of me. I fed and cleaned the horse, in case an SS showed up.

After breakfast I went to the village to pick up my rations, even though I wasn't hungry. There were no SS soldiers around. The prisoners were congregating around the field kitchen, bullshitting about our situation. Everybody had an idea about our fate. One thing we were sure of: servicing the horses was coming to an end.

I soon found Zoli, I told him about the family I stayed with. I told him that I believed the couple would help me escape if I asked. I didn't mention the doctor's visit. I asked Zoli if the situation arrived, would he join me. I didn't think of escaping by myself. My speculation that the couple would help was based on the fact that the housewife brought the doctor, which was a dangerous undertaking in itself. Zoli hesitated, so did I. It sounded too good.

Days went by. We let the escaping idea slip from our minds. We stayed in the village for five days; maybe a week. The wound on my toe healed. I had no more discomfort. On the sixth or seventh day in the village we were ordered to bring the horses, wagons, and all the equipment we had hauled from Plavy, to the village square. All the German overseers and guards were there, including the prisoners. The Germans held an auction. Everything was sold to the peasants.

I don't know how many prisoners escaped, if any, or how many died on the road. It seemed to me there was less than when we started. After the auction, we were assembled and marched to the railroad station. Cattle cars were waiting.

The second time in less than a year I was to enjoy rail travel, compliments of the "Third Reich."

GOING NOWHERE

I think there were only three or four cattle-cars. I can't remember everything. The cattle cars were attached to a train going west. Once in a while the cattle cars were separated from the train and parked on a side track. It didn't take long for the train workers to realize who we were. They cleaned the tracks next to the cattle cars and started to run a locomotive back and forth. Every time they passed they would throw food and cigarettes toward us. The doors of the cattle cars were open. The SS guards walked back and forth. We jumped out from the cattle cars and picked up whatever was on the ground. The Germans didn't interfere. They took the cigarettes (not all) and left the food to us. The actions of the railroad workers lifted our spirits.

The trip lasted forever. By the end of February, or beginning of March, we arrived in Sachsenhausen. The camp commandant refused to accept the shipment. For four days the cattle cars were parked in the camp. The commandant didn't change his mind.

A locomotive was again brought in to take us to the railroad station. From there we were transported to the infamous camp Mauthausen.

As at every camp, the first thing we had to do was take a shower. Never mind that we might have dropped dead from hunger. If so, we had to drop dead clean! Then the barber shop. We were given a designer hair cut. The whole skull was cut with a number ten cutter, it left about quarter of an inch of hair. With the number one cutter, (that cuts the hair very close to the skull), a line in the middle of the head was cut from the front of the forehead, all the way to the neck. It created a stripe we called the "autobahn" (Highway.)

No food yet!

After the barber shop visit we were lined up to get the new numbers. The tattoo from Auschwitz wasn't enough; Mauthausen had its own accounting department. The numbers were stamped on a narrow brass platelet that we had to wear like a bracelet on our left wrist. My number was 136393 or 136339. Just because I don't remember the exact number, doesn't mean I made up the whole story.

120

Meir Barak aka Zoli Berkovic, will vouch for it.

The food wasn't up to par! I was ready to go back to Auschwitz!

Zoli and I were assigned to the same barracks. Some prisoners were taken to work in a stone quarry. We heard all kind of horror stories. Zoli and I didn't work. We were lying around in the sun, telling stories, planning our future, making up imaginary dishes, and killing lice. In the beginning we would clean our cloth, but the lice were multiplying by the thousands if not by the millions. We were losing the battle. The lice started to prevail!

I don't remember how long we stayed in that god-for-saken place. One day in April 1945, we were lined up as usual to be counted. We didn't return to the barracks. We were marched to a meadow surrounded with barbed wire and watch towers. In the middle were six huge tent-like structures. Two thousand of us, all in stripped uniforms, crammed into two tents while the four other tents stayed empty, but just for a short while.

Having nothing to do all day, our minds were constantly occupied with food. There was no food. We got hungrier and hungrier by the minute. With no hope of getting food, we started to chew on grass roots. The grass roots juices quenched our hunger a little, so we started to graze like cows. Soon the green meadow turned yellow. We had eaten all the grass!

The will to survive is a very strange phenomenon. There was no good reason for hope; especially not after the grass was gone. Were we under some hypnotic spell? Were we losing our minds? Were we already crazy?

To be hungry all the time and not be able to think correctly, I wonder why we didn't think of eating the lice!

THEY DIDN'T KNOW WHAT HIT THEM

After a few days of lingering around the tent camp and getting bored, the gates opened. Men in Hungarian military uniforms marched in. Those were the Jews who served with the Hungarian army as slave laborers. To fit with the behavior of Hungarian gentlemen, they marched like soldiers, like the English in the movie "The Bridge over the River Kwai." But they didn't whistle!

We old timers, the striped ones, (they called us the "striped ones" because of our uniforms) lined up at the entrance road to the camp, cheering the Hungarians on. The poor bastards; they didn't know what hit them. They had no inkling about what the hell they were marching into.

Zoli, my childhood friend, and I, stood next to each other and joined in taunting the newcomers. We stopped abruptly. We recognized two familiar figures. They were Zoli's father and his uncle. They also recognized us. They broke ranks and started to hug Zoli, each other, and cry. I stood there and hoped that my father would also be marching in.

He did not!

The four tents filled up in no time. The rest of the newcomers were camping out under the stars. The slave laborers had marched from Hungary and had a little food in their backpacks. They tried to protect what little food they had, but were no match for us 2,000 hungry wolves. Their food disappeared in the most mysterious ways. The Hungarians were cursing and chasing us but didn't dare touch us.

One night a plane flew by and dropped a bomb. Unfortunately the pilot missed its target and the bomb fell in the camp. Some 40 people were killed, and who knows how many were injured? I slept through the whole incident.

It was less than a month before liberation!

A week or two before liberation, we were ordered to pack. To pack what? As I mentioned before, we always traveled light.

We were moving again. The Hungarian slave laborers lined up

122

again as soldiers do. We, the striped ones, marched at the end of the column, clowning around, trying to imitate the Hungarians. And a bunch of clowns we were!

On the road, women prisoners joined the exodus. They looked terrible, maybe worse than we did.

At the villages that we passed, people watched with amazement, but not one dared to approach us, or god forbid, give us a piece of bread. We passed a potato field. The prisoners, like crazies, ran from the formation and dug for potatoes. They ate the potatoes raw. The guards had a hard time restoring order. There was no shooting and no beating. Most of the prisoners who dared to step out from the formation were women.

I salute them!

As darkness fell, we stopped at a meadow close to a forest. I looked for Zoli but to no avail. He was marching with his father and uncle. To look for him was like looking for a needle in a haystack. On the road, two Slovak kids stuck with me. One was 14, and the other, 12 years old.

The idea of getting food from the kitchen didn't look very promising. Roaming on the edge of the forest, I found snails crawling all over. I decided to cook a gourmet dinner. I sent the two kids to find as many snails as possible.

When it came to food, my imagination ran wild. I had never cooked in my life, not even a hardboiled egg. When the kids came back with the snails, I had water boiling in a pot. I dumped the snails into the boiling water. The smell was overwhelming.

We didn't see the German guard approaching. It was too late to grab the pot. The guard kicked the pot. The snail soup spilled, together with the half-cooked snails. Then he made us put out the fire. To make a fire next to the trees wasn't the smartest thing to do.

When the guard left, we picked up the half-cooked snails. Instead of a well made gourmet meal, which we would have preferred, with a little snail soup to wash it down, we had to be satisfied with a medium rare dish. Nobody complained.

Nobody asked for seconds, either. As we were munching on the snails, a young Polish kid approached us. He finished the leftovers and joined our small group.

The next morning we arrived at our destination; another camp. The gate had no welcome sign and the orchestra was absent. The only similarity was the barbed wire fence. I don't think it was electrified.

It seemed to me that the camp had just been erected. We, the striped ones, got the barracks. Most of the Hungarians camped out under the trees. As soon as we arrived, it started to rain. The ground turned into mud. It was hard to walk. The lice were eating us alive. There was hardly any food. People got sick. An epidemic of typhoid broke out. Dead bodies were lying everywhere.

It was the end of April 1945!

The Red Cross delivered a truckload of food. Everybody who could manage to stand on two feet, lined up in front of a building next to the barracks. Standing in the line, I met a schoolmate of mine; Finias. He was originally from Hust in Karpatorussia. We decided to support each other, because everybody was pushing to get to the front. To fall into the mud was as good, as saying good bye to this wonderful world!

The distribution started in an orderly fashion, then, like on a command, the throng started to push. Everybody grabbed whatever their hands reached. The German guards tried to keep the prisoners back with their rifle butts, when this failed, they opened fire. A lot of people were killed. My schoolmate, Finias, was one of them. I came back with empty hands. My two Slovak friends and the Polish kid were also disappointed.

We slept next to each other; actually, more on top of each other. I woke up in the morning, opened my eyes and saw a strange look in my Polish friend's eyes. He was dead!

We heard explosions all day. The day of liberation seemed to be close. We didn't know which army was closing in; Americans, English, or Russians. To us, it made no difference.

I told my two little friends that I am going to escape. Their eyes lit up.

Late the same evening, we saw a commotion. The Hungarians told us that the gate wasn't guarded. We went to investigate. They were right. The guards were gone. We didn't go back to the barracks. The three of us took off in the direction of the explosions.

We were on our way to freedom!

Mazal Tov!

THE AMERICAN PATROL

The two Slovak kids and I moved slowly toward the sound of explosions. From the dark came the words "hands up." Lucky the 12 year old, Robert, understood English. We bumped into three American soldiers on patrol. The soldiers knew that a concentration camp was in the vicinity because they met some other prisoners before they bumped into us. But we were the first ones seen in striped uniforms. The three soldiers emptied their side-packs. We got chocolate, crackers, one orange, and Lucky Strike cigarettes. First we ate all they gave us, then all three of us lit the cigarettes and started to walk in the direction the soldiers directed us.

The concentration camp was near a town called Gunskirchen. To walk the 11 miles from Gunskirchen to Wells, took us most of the night. It was dark when we hit the outskirts of Wells. An American soldier directed us to a house and told us to go up to the attic. In the attic we met Hungarians that had arrived before us, munching on bread. There was no need to beg. There was enough bread for an army.

With full stomachs, and knowing we were free, we fell into a peaceful sleep. In the morning, I started to rummage around the attic. I found German military helmets, gas masks, bayonets, bread, cans with fat, and many more things. I tore out the leather liner from the helmet, to use as a pot. For breakfast, I served deep-fried bread.

I have no inkling why I came up with the stupid idea to deep fry bread. After a whole year of not having any fats, all three of us got sick, sitting on the toilet, the rest of the day.

The night that we left, the German guards had returned and kept the prisoners from leaving the camp. Next day the American Army liberated the camp. The few hundred prisoners that survived were pouring into the city. The Americans surrounded us, took away our uniforms, sprayed us with DDT and cleaned us up. They had no replacement for our uniforms. They couldn't dress us in American uniforms, so they gave us whatever they found, mostly discarded German garb. I had a coat from the Luftwaffe (German Air Force). It was at least three sizes to large. But who cared?

The first few days after liberation, we were housed next to an abandoned airfield. The airfield was surrounded with three story buildings. My two friends and I checked out every room. There was nothing useful to be found. The prisoners who hit the buildings before us made sure nothing useful was left.

The happiness lasted only a few days. First the 14 year old got sick. We took him to the hospital. Than Robert, the 12 year old got sick. I took him to the hospital. A day later I checked in with high fever. It was diagnosed as typhoid.

The lice had done their job. And what a thorough job they did! I remember very little about my stay in the hospital. Most of the time, I was delirious. One thing I remember vividly: two German officers, clad in white robes, were explaining my situation to an American officer, who wore a helmet. They waved their hand, like saying, nothing can be done. The American nodded.

How wrong they were! Two weeks later I was able to walk, without help, to the bathroom. A large mirror was on the wall. I turned around to see who is behind me. I didn't recognize myself. I had survived! I was sixteen years old

RECUPERATING

At the end of May 1945, I was shipped to a new place. It was somewhere close to the city of Wells. The place was close to an airfield. It seemed that this neighborhood had airfields everywhere. German pilots had occupied the buildings, but it was now converted to a recuperation center under the supervision of American military doctors. The crew consisted of German doctors and nurses. Some of the doctors wore their Nazi uniforms, including all their decorations. The difference was now we were dictating the rules.

And a big difference it was!

The airport was used to fly the ex-prisoners home. Planes landed and took off 24 hours a day. People from all over Europe were concentrated at this facility; from Netherlands, Belgium, Yugoslavia, Italy, France, and who knows how many other countries. The repatriates were housed temporarily in the hangars. The food was supplied by the American military: canned food, powdered milk, chocolates, cigarettes, and all the goodies in the world. The ex-prisoners boarding the planes had to leave everything behind.

The diet at the recuperating center was very strict. In the beginning, we were fed whatever was available. A lot of ex-prisoners got sick because their systems were not able to digest any fatty foods. The doctors therefore insisted on a very lean diet. This made us hungry. To supplement our ration we went to the airport to scavenge.

I was recuperating slowly. I felt that with my walking stick I could make it to the airport. The trip was for nothing. I got a small piece of chocolate from a Yugoslav man. I asked for cigarettes, but he told me I am too young to smoke and gave me none.

It was a balmy day. On my way back, I decided to stop at the brook and rest. It was so peaceful. Listening to the rumbling of the brook, I fell asleep. The night nurse found my bed empty. A search party was organized. In no time they found me sleeping under a tree.

I felt feverish. Next morning the attending doctor checked my lungs and suspected something worse than a common cold. He asked the American doctor to see me. The American doctor wasted no time. He put me in his jeep and drove me to a hospital in Wells. After xrays were taken I was given a bed in one of the wards.

The next day, the same American doctor came to see me. He told me that I have lung tuberculosis and need immediate treatment. He told me, that for the time being I shall stay in Wells until he finds a hospital where I can be properly treated.

Only one ex-prisoner was in the ward, the rest were American soldiers. The ex-prisoner was a Polish Jew. He received blood transfusions. From my bed I saw how the blood slowly dripped into his veins. I never saw anything like it before in my life. It was fascinating. The floor nurse passed every few minutes checking the transfusion. After looking at the patient she rushed out of the ward and returned quickly with a doctor. The doctor checked the Polish man, pulled the needle from his vein and pronounced him dead.

The poor guy was soon carried out. The nurse came to my bed with a bottle of yellow liquid. She hung the bottle over my head and the doctor came to insert the needle in my arm. Watching the Polish man expiring in the middle of the transfusion I assumed that all the liquid must enter my vein, otherwise good bye cruel world.

I didn't take my eye off the bottle, watching the liquid slowly dripping into my emaciated body.

It took forever!

When the nurse came to remove the needle from my arm I gave her a big smile. She couldn't guess the significance of it. She couldn't read my mind. A couple of days later I got another bottle of the same yellow liquid. This time I wasn't concerned. I was sure they were saving my life.

About a week or so later, the same doctor that brought me to the hospital in Wells picked me up in his jeep and drove me to Linz. In Linz, a lung specialist took over. The treatment I was given isn't used any more. The procedure was called pneumothorax. A large needle was inserted between the ribs. It was pushed in until it punctured the pleura. Air was pumped between the pleura and the lung. The procedure made the lung work less. It was believed that by giving the lung some rest it would heal the wound created by tuberculosis and prevent it from spreading.

Don't quote me. I am not a doctor. Nor am I a writer!

Uncle Joe Judd was an American soldier. He served under General Mark Clark. With his unit he fought his way from Africa all the way to Austria. Joe found my name on the list of the survivors. He started to look for me. He drove his jeep from place to place, trying to find me. Every time he came to a place where I was supposed to be, he was told that I had been transferred to another place. Joe didn't give up. He chased a bus that carried me to Czechoslovakia. The Russian border guards wouldn't let him enter the country. He had to wait another six months to see me.

I recuperated well. The doctor thought I was well enough to travel. It was August 1945. We traveled in a group of 12. Because the Americans ran out of clothes, they dressed us in clothing used by the German pilots. I got a gray jacket without a collar or buttons. It had a string that could be used to keep the jacket closed. The pants were supposed to be tucked into the boots, but because we had no boots, the pants legs hung in a strange way. The hats completed the circus-like attire. We wore all kinds of German military hats. Not one of the 12 was the same. When we arrived at the railroad station in Prague, a group of Russian soldiers asked us to exchange our hats for their military boot caps. We were only too happy to oblige.

The people in the streets of Prague were unreal. They pushed money and food stamps in our hands. They hugged us and cried.

It was a welcome I hadn't counted on!

I felt great! I was free. I was home!

THE HOSPITAL IN PRAGUE

All returnees from the camps signed in at an office at the railroad station. The nurse who read my file that I brought with me from Linz, instructed a helper to take me to an infirmary. There, a young doctor checked the file and told me I must stay for a few days, and will be hospitalized. He told me not to worry, and assured me that he will arrange a place where I will receive the appropriate treatment.

A couple of days later, an ambulance took me to a hospital located on the banks of the Vltava River.

Before being assigned to a room, I was examined by a tall, middle aged, very good looking, medical specialist. The man had movie star quality, and was a lung specialist to boot. I was ushered into a room that had only two beds. My roommate was also a camp survivor. He was a Polish Jew, named Jankl. Having spent a year in Poland, I had no problem communicating with him. Jankl was older than I, more experienced, and much smarter.

We had hit it off from the first minute.

While in the hospital, I wrote two letters to my village; Zdana. One was addressed to my mother. I believed there was an outside chance that she had survived. The next day, after we arrived from our liberation from Birkenau, I had an opportunity to talk to my girlfriend; blonde, blue eyed, freckle faced, Hanna, whom I met at the brick factory. She had told me she was in the same group with my mother.

The first day in the concentration camps was the most crucial. Chosen to work was the only chance to stay alive, but for how long? That was a different question!

My father was killed as a slave laborer on the Russian front before we were taken to the concentration camp. My brother was too young to survive the first day in the camp, so ended the rest of my family. They were too old or they had children. In both cases their lives ended in the gas chambers!

I wrote the second letter to my nanny, Katka Veresova, a Catholic. Her chances to survive were guaranteed by her religion!

A month went by. I had no answer from my mother or my

130

nanny.

The treatment in Prague continued the same way it was administered in Linz. Twice a week I was pumped with air, and twice a week I was examined under a fluoroscope. With the radiation I received from those treatments I should glow in the dark. The doctor in the Prague hospital wasn't satisfied with the results. He contemplated using more invasive treatments. Because I was a teenager, the procedure required a parent's signature. The surgeon wanted to cut out four of my ribs. It would have crippled me for life. The surgeon, having no way to contact my parents, decided to get my signature.

The head nurse became interested in my well being. It went beyond professional duties. It became very personal. She inquired about everything; my parents, my schooling, and my experience in the camps. She would sit next to my bed for hours after her shift ended. When she found out what the surgeon wanted to do, she decided to intervene. She didn't beat around the bush. She told me that what she will tell me has to be a secret between the two of us. If anybody ever finds out what she plans to tell me, she would be fired on the spot, and no hospital in all Czechoslovakia would hire her.

First, she asked me if I heard from my mother. I told her I have no news from her or from the other villagers. I told her that I suspect my whole family was wiped out.

The words of her plan rang in my ears. "I know what the surgeon wants you to sign. I am not a doctor, but I am a nurse for thirty years. I have a lot of experience and you are so young. The procedure the doctor wants to perform on you would cripple you for life. It is irreversible! Don't agree to the operation."

She had tears in her eyes. I sensed that something more is coming. She told me that she is living alone and if I agree, she would like to adopt me. Not thinking for a minute, I agreed.

My situation changed drastically. The relationship between nurse and patient became more like a mother and a sick child. I recuperated beyond anybody's imagination. I hung out in the hospital, visiting other survivors and talking to anybody who wanted to listen. I went to bed only at the prescribed time.

Around the six or seventh week in the hospital, my adopted mother-nurse, came to my room. It was not unusual for her to drop by any time of day. I saw her eyes were red. I knew she had been crying.

She asked me to get up and come with her. I was afraid to ask where. I thought maybe the surgeon had found a way to circumvent the need for me to sign the necessary papers, and decided to proceed with the operation.

It wasn't the surgeon we were to see. It was my mother and my cousin, Andrew Rauchman who waited in the corridor.

My mother had received my letter about a month after I wrote it. A few days before the liberation, she learned from Zoli and his father, who saw me in the Gunskirchen camp, that I was alive. But they had no idea as to my whereabouts. My mother never forgave Lajos Berkovic; Zoli's father, for not taking care of me. She was wrong. I had disappeared from the camp a day before the liberation, so Zoli and his father had no idea what happened to me. When Zoli and his father were liberated the next day, I was already spending time on the toilet, from eating the deep fried bread.

With the surgeon's permission, I was discharged from the hospital. He gave my file to my mother and advised her to take me to a sanatorium to recuperate. The trip from Prague to Slovakia was horrendous. The trains were slow, I had a low grade fever, and we ran out of food. Not withstanding all the difficulties, we finally arrived at Novy Smovec in the Tatry Mountains.

Through Andrew's cousin, Eva's, connections, I was admitted to the sanatorium. The Czechoslovak government picked up the bill. Not long ago, one government tried to eliminate me. Now, a different one tried to save me.

Go Figure!

THE SANATORIUM

I stayed in a room with six beds, and doors that opened to a balcony with six cots. One cot for each patient, with a sleeping bag lined with fur, and a zipper that you could close all the way up to your eyeballs. My bed inside, was on the north side of the room. From it I could see the surrounding forest; all pine trees. In early morning, fog would cover the valley. It felt like being high above everything, distanced from all the problems; from the world that brought so much misery to so many people.

I was the only holocaust survivor in the room: two Czechs, three Slovaks, and me, the Slovak Jew!

Life in the sanatorium was monotonous. Most of the patients were older. We youngsters were never bored. The discipline could be compared only to the military. At that time, the medical profession in Czechoslovakia believed that lots of rest, good food, and the few procedures available, were the best chance for the patients to regain health.

There were four periods in the day that we had to be in bed. We had the choice to rest in the sleeping bags, on the balcony, or in bed in our rooms with open doors. From eight to ten in the morning, the doctor in charge, moved from room to room to see his patients. Between two and four in the afternoon was the quiet period. There was no talking then, playing cards, or chess. From seven to nine in the evening we were permitted to spend our time playing chess, billiards, reading, or conversing with other patients.

As I mentioned, the discipline was very strict. One strike and the patient was out. If caught smoking a cigarette it took less then half an hour to be shipped out of the sanatorium.

The medical attention was not that far behind the discipline. Three times a day our temperature was measured and recorded. The doctor saw us every day, including Sundays. I was treated with the pneumothorax, twice a week. I was examined under a fluoroscope before the treatment and after. I was x-rayed once a month for three years. I was given calcium shots. The blood sedimentation was checked once a month. The only uncomfortable treatment was the calcium shots and those only had a strange effect when injecting too fast. The feeling was that you are making in your pants. My doctor was female. Most embarrassing!

With all the radiation I got it's a wonder I don't glow in the middle of the day. Only kidding! On the other hand, it might have killed every cancer cell in my body.

Next to my bed, was a patient from a small town in Slovakia. He was a merchant. A small man; fragile, and probably very sick. He told jokes all the time. He hardly finished one, when he told another one. We were roaring with laughter all the time, until one day he gagged, laughing on his own joke, and dropped dead.

What a way to go!

From the beginning, my social life evolved around the people I knew from home. My uncle Moritz Rauchman and his niece were on the first floor. I befriended Alex Treiber, Oscar Schlesinger, a guy named Herskovitz; a girl named Mermelstein, and one more girl whose name escapes me. In our free time we hung out together. No wonder. We were all veterans of Auschwitz, and Jews, to boot.

Joe Judd, my uncle, was an American soldier now serving in Austria. In the fall of 1945 he came to visit his sister; my mother, and the rest of the family including me. Joe was very upset about how I looked. My mother brought shirts and pants that were a little bit big for me. Uncle Joe probably thought that I looked like a clown. I didn't care. After the stripped pajamas everything looked good to me.

Not to Uncle Joe!

I don't remember taking any measurements, but he must have, because on his Christmas vacation he brought three American military uniforms made to my measure: shirts, underwear, socks, cigarettes, (not to smoke, only to use as currency) Italian salamis, and best of all: Swiss chocolates.

The American uniform created a miracle. I walked as a rooster among the hens. Even the young nurses paid attention. It wasn't me, it was the American cigarettes: Chesterfields, Lucky Strikes, and the Swiss chocolate that stimulated their nostrils.

Uncle Joe arranged a permit to take me for a week vacation to visit my family. Joe's rank was Master Sergeant. It was his fourth year in the army. His uniform was full of stripes, medals, and insignia. In Slovakia he could have been mistaken for a general. The Slovak soldiers in the street, including the officers, saluted him.

134

We went to Humenne to see my new aunt, Arlene, (Joe had married her) and my cousin Gary. At the same time, I visited my Uncle Joe Roth, his wife Ilonka, and my cousins, Ervin and Aliska (she was in Birkenau from 1942). I also met my childhood friend, Zoli Berkovic. This was our first meeting since being separated in Gunskirchen. Walking in the street in Humenne with Zoli and Ervin, I met Odze; the foreman in stable two, who slapped my face for not obeying his order. He asked me if I wanted to return the slap. I refused. We shook hands.

Back in the sanatorium, I found my room empty. All the patients were dismissed or transferred to different rooms. I had the room to myself. The night nurse, who was six years older than I, liked Swiss chocolates, and I liked her. She visited my room often to tend to my well being, and satisfy her hunger for chocolates.

My health improved remarkably. I gained weight, grew six inches, and had no low grade fever that patients with tuberculosis usually have.

I looked and felt healthy!

My doctor had the same opinion and was ready to discharge me. Uncle Joe convinced the doctor that another three months in the sanatorium would improve my health. For two cartons of Lucky Strikes, the doctor agreed with Uncle Joe's diagnosis.

I was transferred to the fifth floor. I spent the last three months in the sanatorium with a very nice young boy from Humenne. We played chess every opportunity we had. He also helped me regain command of the Slovak language.

By the end of April 1946, I was discharged from the sanatorium with a recommendation to continue the treatment received, for another two years.

Those last two years were tough. Before then wasn't a picnic either!

BACK TO SQUARE ONE

I was now in Kosice, the town I knew well. The town I went to school in for four years. But now I was a stranger. I didn't know who, if any, of my classmates survived, and who perished. Walking in a street one afternoon I bumped into a schoolmate from Budapest. I was happy to see a familiar face. I thought maybe he could give me some information about our other classmates. I was disappointed to hear that he was only visiting and that he had continued his studies in Budapest. I roamed the streets hoping to meet somebody; anybody; friend or foe. It made no difference. I was lost. I had no idea in which direction to turn. My father was gone. My uncles and aunts were gone. And the youth organization that I had belonged to was no longer there.

I learned that one of my closest friends, Laci Roth, was shot dead with his father on the shores of the Danube River. Roaming the streets, I bumped into another of my friends, at least I thought so: Gabi Reich. We hugged. We kissed. And we cried. In our senior year, we were as close as Siamese twins. We had spent all of our free time together. I did his math homework and he wrote my essays for literature class. I was on my way to an interview. He was in hurry to meet somebody. We arranged to meet on the same spot, the next day. I couldn't sleep, I was so happy. All my worries were gone. Gabi was a city kid. He could help me. Next day, as agreed, I arrived early. We had agreed to meet at two in the afternoon, but I couldn't wait. I was there before one. Two o'clock arrived and no Gabi. By four I began to think Gabi won't come. I waited until eight in the evening. I went home with tears in my eyes. I never saw him again. It was like two ships passing in the night.

My mother had rented a room on Zvonarska Street. It was a single room with a separate entrance. I was too old to share a room with my mother. The apartment had three more bedrooms. My mother rented one for me. The other two were occupied by the landlady, her younger sister, and a niece. I didn't mind sharing a bedroom with any of the ladies, but only the sister, five years my senior, showed any interest. Unfortunately, she shared the room with the niece, so the whole idea of sharing a bed with her was only a dream of a budding young lad.

A kosher deli was in the same building, facing the street. It had a game room with two billiard tables. I was a better than average player. I got involved with some unsavory characters and joined the gamblers in a, not the cleanest, gambling scheme. The deli's proprietor, who knew my mother, tipped her off. He told her about the group I hung around with.

In the deli, I met a man, Mr. Namlik, that I had some dealings with in the camps. Actually, he was my connection to sell the potatoes that I had smuggled into the camp. He was as happy to see me as I was to see him. He offered me a job. He wanted me to join him in a black market deal in sugar that he was involved in. I would have joined him, but the offer was contingent on entering into a homosexual relationship with him.

I wasn't that desperate.

My brain was empty. I wasn't thinking. I wasn't hungry anymore. My brain was in a holding pattern. For a long time the stomach had dictated my brain's function. Now I was 17 plus. It was time to switch the dictating.

I had to get a jolt from the outside. My mother was smart. Now I can admit it. She did not confront me about my behavior. She didn't volunteer to enlighten me with the information she received from the deli proprietor. Instead, she hinted that it might be possible for me to get a job in a factory. Where did she get that knowledge to handle me with such reversed psychology? Or was it only common sense? She probably anticipated an outburst, me throwing a shit fit, or screaming bloody murder.

Nothing of the kind!

I was a spoiled brat, only a year out of the concentration camps. How soon we forget! My American uniform: the Lucky Strike cigarettes, the chocolate, and money in the pocket. What else could a 17 year old bum dream of? Ah, girls, girls, girls!

I did not rebel. I didn't throw a shit fit, and I didn't scream bloody murder. I agreed to see the owner of the factory the next day.

I arrived at the factory on time, where I met Mr. Nrets, and his partner, Mr. Namdirf. The former was an older man; maybe in his fifties. He had a four or five day old beard, looked dirty, wore a collar-less white shirt that was more gray than white. His belly bulged out over his pants that bore no belt. He sweated like a pig with an unpleasant odor. To me he was a white gorilla. I was ready to turn and run.

I did not.

He introduced me to his partner, Namdirf, and took me into his office. The office was no improvement over Mr. Nrets. The walls were dirty. The single window looked as though it had never been washed. The floor was indescribable. The tables were littered with papers. A real mess! Was I destined to work in these conditions? Was this my future?

Mother Nature, Mother Roth, please help me!

Mr. Nrets asked me if I know any bookkeeping. Bookkeeping? "Yes, Mr. Nrets. I did some in school, but I am a bit rusty, having been out of circulation for the past two years." I lied.

"Do not worry." He said. "I'll teach it to you in no time."

And so he did.

Mr. Nrets did the bookkeeping for a very short time, because for any practical purposes, he was an illiterate. He could hardly write a number in three squares, rather than one. The entry book was a mess. On my first day I had to rewrite all the pages that he did. It took a week to redo all that he did. He was, however, an excellent teacher. By the third month, I was independent and on my own. At the same time, the Czech government was going Communist. And the tax department was sending new instructions daily.

Mr. Nrets did not speak Slovak. He couldn't understand those instructions and he became more dependent on me. I became not only a bookkeeper, but also a translator. Because of the Tax Department's new rules, we were forced to hire more people. I became the elder statesman in the office before reaching age eighteen.

My head swelled. A local manufacturer, who did business with our company, saw our books. He liked my handwriting so much he offered me a job with his company at a salary three times what I was making. I felt obligated to Mr. Nrets, and to his wife who was my mother's friend. I didn't quit, but I did ask for a raise. I asked for the same amount the other manufacturer had offered. Nrets thought that amount was too high. He offered to double my salary. I accepted.

I was on cloud nine. I was less than 18 years old and I was the highest paid employee in the factory.

Mr. Nrets didn't draw a salary. He dipped into the cash register in a very unorthodox manner. Every large order was split in two. As soon as the first half arrived, the papers for both parts disappeared. The shipment was paid in cash and the money pocketed by Nrets and, probably, his partner, Namdirf.

The second part was legitimate and it was entered in the books as such. The merchandise sold without the invoice was placed on the black market. This way the inventory was always correct. The tax people had no knowledge of the operation. And I kept my mouth shut. It didn't make me proud!

That wasn't the only talent Mr. Nrets had.

We manufactured small boxes for envelopes. First a form was cut and than stitched to form a box. I would stand with a stopwatch in my hand and count how many stitches a worker made in a certain time. Before I finished the calculation Mr. Nrets would give me the number. If he ever missed, which was seldom, it wasn't by more than a fraction of a penny. The White Gorilla was a genius.

Go figure!

FREDDY KARP

I don't believe in destiny, but I have a difficult time explaining a meeting with Freddy Karp, and its aftermath. He and I were classmates in junior high school. He was a year older. He wasn't the athletic type; therefore I had little contact with him. When I met him on the street in Kosice, after the war, I never dreamed that such an accidental meeting would change the course of my life. Our talk was casual; asking about classmates and our own situation, and plain bullshit.

Freddy asked me if I continued with my soccer career. I was surprised that he even remembered me playing soccer in junior high. I told him that I was in a sanatorium for a whole year, but I had just signed up with a small club in the mountains. He told me that he belongs to an organization that has a lot of young kids who want to play soccer. And they need a coach. He asked me to consider being a coach for those kids. Then and there I agreed to take the job. We agreed to meet in his clubhouse a week later.

I anticipated meeting all those kids, but when I arrived, there were no kids to be seen. Freddy told me there was a mix up and the kids won't be coming. There were young guys and gals in attendance. Freddy introduced them to me, one by one. He told me they are to have a meeting and will listen to a lecture. If I feel like it, he said I could stay and participate.

The clubhouse had a Ping-Pong table. One of the gals asked me to play. I told her that I had never played. Her name was Aliska.

"Never mind," she said. "I shall teach you."

It was a set up. The organization didn't have a soccer club and they didn't need a coach. Freddy tried to get me to join the organization. At this time I was completely apolitical. I agreed to come the following week for one of their meetings.

I was really an eyesore at the club. They wore no hats or neckties. They didn't smoke and they abstained from intimate relationships. I was the opposite. They had an agenda. I never expected that I was to be worked on. Week after week I changed my old image and slowly became one of them.

140

I started reading books that the organization recommended. I met some older members that were a part of the leadership, under the tutelage of an Israeli representative of the political party called Hashomer Hatzair. Maybe I was indoctrinated, maybe not. I liked the young people. I liked their enthusiasm. I liked the books they read. I liked the way they danced, the way they sang. In a word, I liked it all.

My mother was planning to immigrate to the USA but I thought nothing would come of it. Because of the red tape it would take a long time. And her visa and immigration papers had yet to arrive. I decided to join the organization. I became friendly with one of the gals. She was two years older than I. We hung out together until I made a stupid decision and introduced her to my mother. My mother took her aside and described me as a womanizer and a skirt chaser. She hoped that I would leave the organization and immigrate with her to the States. As a woman, she understood that if I got too involved with some gal, her chances would be slimmer of convincing me to go with her. Those were her thoughts. And that was her agenda. But I wasn't a womanizer and I didn't chase skirts. I was always loyal to the gals I hung out with.

I was introduced to a new girl. She was a woman, rather than a girl. Oh God, why must I have a new friend? If she had joined a month earlier I would have chased her. Her name was Katka Frankova. I had heard that name before, but couldn't remember where or when. I had to wait 40 years to get the answer. Much later, I visited Katka in Israel. She introduced me to her friend, Vanda Kardos. I asked Vanda if she had a younger brother, Egon.

She said, "Yes, why do you ask?"

Egon had been my classmate.

I didn't elaborate.

When in junior high, Egon promised to introduce us boys to his sister's girlfriends. We were supposed to meet at a certain time, a block away from where the girls were meeting. The girls were two years older than we. They were half-baked women, with boobs to match. Not waiting for an introduction, we ran away. That's how I knew Katka's name.

To get back to Freddy Karp and his group, the organization decided to put on a show about the life in a Kibbutz. Katka got the leading female part and as luck would have it, I got the leading male part. It wasn't so much the acting that I was excited about. The part, at one point, called for a kiss on the lips. That was more then I could ask for. Nothing came of the kiss. At the rehearsals it was make believe, but I was sure that I would have the opportunity on the stage. Nothing came of it. She turned her head, and I only kissed her on the cheek. Talk about disappointment. Forty years later, I kissed her on the lips at our wedding. Katka Frankova is now my wife.

By the spring of 1947, the organization decided to train people to make costume jewelry. Two gals and I were chosen to attend a specialized school to learn the trade. Ishka Treitel was supposed to learn design, Ruth Neuman was to learn gilding, and I, the manufacturing technique.

The organization had a commune in Liberec, a town close to the school we were to attend. I was shipped out to Liberec to take a test. All three of us passed and were to start our studies in September 1947. I went back to Kosice to spend the rest of the summer. The first thing I did there: I went to see my girl friend. To my chagrin I found that my girl friend had a boy friend. It seemed that only I thought of her as a girl friend. I was heart broken. But my broken heart healed very fast. Maybe it never broke. How does a broken heart feel, anyway?

Two weeks later I was on my way back to Liberec. As soon as I arrived, I was told that the studies in the school were postponed. I had to look for a job, preferably in a jewelry factory. I went to Jablonec, the city where all the costume jewelry factories were located. I landed a job the same day. So did one of the gals named Gila. Two of us got the job in the same factory. I was assigned to a stamping machine. I think Gila started at the gilding department. It was a small factory of 50 or so employees. The president or the "Top Comrade" belonged to the Communist Party and so did most of the workers.

World War II had ended only two years before and all necessities were in short supply, if any. But in the factory we got separate rations of cigarettes, shoes, food, and all kind of items not available to the public. Relatively speaking, we were in a more pleasant situation than the people who didn't belong to the union or the party. Gila and I couldn't join the party because we were Zionist and had our own associations. But because we were considered left wing Socialist, belonging to a non-Communist Party was considered an aberration, so we were treated as if we were one of them.

Every worker assigned to production was given a quota. We worked 11 hours a day, five days a week. At the end of the week the workers assembled to evaluate the week's production. Those who exceeded the quota were praised and given bonuses. The work was tedious. Concentration had to be at the maximum. One false move and your fingers were gone.

I learned how there was a possibility to reduce the danger and also be able to knock out more forms at the same time. I asked the foreman to change the way to cut pieces by my machine. He hesitated. He was afraid the waste will increase and he will be accused of irresponsibility. I convinced him otherwise. I predicted a 100% increase in production. I told him it would us make us look good in the eyes of management and the money will be twofold.

The foreman was a wise man. He cautioned me to slow down. He said, "How long do you think you will be able to work at that pace?"

I paid no attention. I wanted praise. I wanted to be a "Stahkanovite." I wanted to make more money, not for myself, but for the commune. I was almost 18 years old! Within a week of my new approach on the stamping machine, I doubled my quota. By the end of the month I was up to staggering numbers. My weekly pay was more than the president's. This had to be stopped. The quota was changed and increased. Now there were days when I couldn't even reach the hundred percent.

From being a top worker, I became just an average worker, playing with the possibility of being called a saboteur. This is the weakness of the system. The initiative to be creative was curtailed. The system tried to eliminate the "Being" to create a "Thing." It did not work. It can never work.

The commune itself was located on the outskirts of the city of Liberec. We occupied two floors. Five or six of us guys shared the larger rooms, and two or three, the smaller ones. The gals had separate rooms. It didn't take long for my broken heart to heal. The heart mending gal, a kitchen worker, was a healthy blonde; pretty in her own way. She was a fencer and kept an epee in the kitchen. Her name was Zlata. To make the story short, we got involved. The rules were clear. The group was scheduled to go to Palestine, most probably on illegal ships. Intimate relationships were out of the question. I was ready to obey all kind of rules but not this one. Zlata had the same opinion. For a while we were able to keep our relationship under the rug. Soon one of the gals became aware of it and we were afraid she would tell on us. We had only one choice. We couldn't continue our relationship in the commune, we therefore decided to leave. We promised each other to love forever, and parted with a plan to meet soon. I went back to Kosice, and Zlata went to live with her sister in Slovakia.

I was back in Kosice, and out of the commune, while my mother began making arrangements for my immigration to the States. Because she was getting married to an American veteran, I too, was eligible for an immigration visa. My mother had to be in the States no later than December 1947, and my papers couldn't be finished by then. I was left alone in Kosice. I inherited her apartment and had a substantial amount of money. More money soon came from the States. The exchange rate at the time was so much in favor of the dollar that $500 made me the richest kid in town.

I was scheduled to depart for the States at the end of March or beginning of April. The paper work progressed and we were pretty well set for me being in the USA before the start of the school year.

My five years older cousin lived in Kosice with two of his friends. They dealt in contraband. The trio belonged to a group of smugglers transporting cigarettes from Hungary to Czechoslovakia. On the return trip they brought silk stockings, ladies underwear, and what ever else that were part of the barter. The Russian soldiers, on the border between the two countries, were paid off handsomely to look the other way.

To avoid having to pay off the local police, the guys used me to deliver cartons of cigarettes in the city. They gave me their motorcycle to ride. That was enough of a payoff since I had plenty of money.

My cousin wanted to use my apartment for a tryst with a prostitute. I went to the movies and it was agreed that by a certain time he would vacate the room. One evening I came home while the two were still in the room, not ready to leave. The prostitute was a young, good looking woman. I talked her into staying. She must have been at least ten years older than me. I treated her like a girl friend. I

144

walked her home every time she came to see me. I bought her gifts. I took her to the movies. She took a liking to me. I had a free ride for the next four months.

I was free. I had money and plenty of time on my hands.

I didn't short change myself. I purchased a pair of skis, a nice ski outfit, boots made to order, and everything else to look good. Then I took off for the ski resort in the Tatry Mountains. I planned to stay for at least two weeks. I made a reservation in a small lodge close to the slopes. The first evening at dinner, I sat alone. I was early; the other guests had yet to arrive for dinner. I struck up a conversation with the waitress named Jana. She spoke Czech. She was a student from Bmo. I asked her if she skied. "Yes." She said. That's why she came to the mountains to be a waitress. I asked her if she would like to join me on her day off. Jana was very happy to accept the invitation. I made it clear to her that I will pick up the tab. The next day, she managed to get the day off. I suggested that we go to the ski slope next to the lodge. It was a mild slope and I was a real beginner. I told her so.

Jana told me that she is also a beginner, but she knows a much better place, about six miles away. We packed our gear and took the train to the slope of her choice. I did not dream of the predicament I was drawn into. The slope had only one lift. It took forever to reach the top of the mountain. As soon as we arrived, she strapped the skis to her boots and off she went. The slope was steep. It was for experts, surely not for beginners. I fell all over. I looked more like a snowman than a skier. I don't remember how I ever got to the bottom. She had a great time. I made sure to have a great time with her in a sport of my choice. I stayed in the lodge for three weeks.

At the end of March, three of my friends; Jaffa Kroll (a girl) Efraim Leizon, and Zev Apotheker, came to Kosice. They hoped to get help from the Jewish community. How disappointed they must have been to learn that in the Jewish community nobody gave a damn about their plight. It was cruel and demeaning to send their own members begging, when at the same time, the heads of the organization spent thousands.

I got in touch with my cousin, Andrew Rauchmann, who had connections with the black marketers. I took good care of Jaffa. I bought everything she needed that I could put my hands on, including underwear and bras. I paid dearly for it. I was teased for years about the bras.

In the USA, my uncle Harry Judd, decided that I should see a little of the world before I came to the States. I was supposed to go to Paris, Rio, and Mexico City, where he was supposed to pick me up. I took a train to Prague to arrange all the necessary visas. By the end of March 1948, I had all the necessary papers. The start of the journey was scheduled for the beginning of April.

There was one more job scheduled for me before my departure that I wasn't aware of. I met Freddy Karp in the street. Was he the Devil himself, or my Angel? Who knows? I'm certain Freddy didn't plan to involve me. If he had, he would have sought me out in my apartment. He knew where I lived. He must have been desperate to find somebody to pull off the job, and I just happened to fly into his net.

He knew that I planned to go the States, but as an ex-member of the organization, and as a favor for old time's sake, he had this job for me. He told me that there were four people in town that have to be taken to Bratislava from Kosice. The foursome: two women and two men who are in town illegally and have to be accompanied, because they have no papers and don't speak Slovak. I don't have to be concerned. Everything is arranged. I was asked to come to a meeting Saturday afternoon where I will get my instructions. Freddy told me not to ask questions. All I have to know is I had to accompany four people from Kosice to Bratislava. Basta! Are you game? Sure, no sweat! If I had thought for two more minutes, I would have said no. But that wouldn't have been me. With me a word is a word! A handshake is a handshake! If a lot of crap had to be eaten later, so be it.

That wasn't the first time I volunteered at the spur of the moment, and it wouldn't be the last time. And the price was getting much higher. I never learned. It was a question of honor. Or was it?

There was no meeting. It was Freddy with the instructions. Sunday afternoon at two, I had to appear at the railroad station in Kosice. I was supposed to buy six tickets for a second class coach on the express train to Bratislava. I had to board the train alone and pay off the conductor to reserve the coach for us. We were only five but the coach had six seats, therefore, not to compromise the conductor, all six seats were paid for.

As soon as I finished that task I had to appear at the window and signal Freddy that the first stage of the mission was completed. I got off the train to meet Freddy and the four passengers. At the station, I saw many members of the organization. They were scattered all over the platform. Freddy told me that I was asked to do the job because the police might get suspicious if they saw members of the organization with strangers.

Was it a diversion? Or were they making sure the "four" are on their way. I was told to take the first couple to the train, put Slovak newspapers in their hand, to make believe they are local people and then return to the platform and pick up the second couple. I did.

Walking with the second couple, I saw the first couple standing in front of the coach with a policeman. I immediately realized there is trouble. There was no backing out. I had to get rid of the second couple but at that point, Freddy disappeared.

What the hell am I doing here? The first secret job I get and I botched it up before it started. I wasn't trained for this! I was an amateur! No James Bond.

On the platform, I recognized one gal. She belonged to the younger group of our organization. I didn't know she was a lookout. I thought to return to her and ask her to take care of the couple. At once I saw an older man, the father of a friend of mine. I approached him. "Mr. Znah," I said, "Do not ask questions. Take the couple. They only speak Yiddish. Make sure they arrive at the address on the paper with the tickets I just shoved in your palm. And God help you. Do you understand?" I didn't know then that Mr. Znah was a pro.

I approached the policeman with my couple. I made believe to translate, but what I really did was try to pay off the policeman. I thought he would accept, because I saw some hesitation on his face. But he took us to the police station. I was booked, my passport was confiscated, and I was placed in an adjacent room. The couple was questioned, but I had no way of knowing what was happening. I saw the policeman that brought us in, leave. Where he went, I couldn't tell. After being incarcerated in the concentration camps I wasn't too keen about being locked up again. So I left the room where the cop had placed me and boarded the train. I waited until the train pulled out from the station and then went to look for Mr. Znah. I found him in a coach with my couple. It was smooth sailing all the way to Bratislava. At the station, I took a cab, unloaded the couple at the address I was given, and ran to the headquarters of my ex-organization.

I didn't have to do too much explanation. I was given a train ticket and was on my way to the commune in Liberec. I met all my old friends. I couldn't go back to Kosice. My passport was gone and there was no way to retrieve it. I was a fugitive. The "Organization" decided to ship me out of the country at the first opportunity. About a week later I was on my way to West Germany.

The couple that was arrested in Kosice was freed the next day.

It cost a bundle!

GOING WEST SECOND ROUND

Our group of 12 young men and women traveled by train to a town on the Czech-German border. From there, we traveled by trucks to our new destination, a camp operated under the auspices of the Hagana. There I realized that I had volunteered for the soon to be established army of the state of Israel. I became a volunteer, without volunteering.

In the camp, there were young people from all over Europe. Polish, Russian, Hungarian, Slovaks, and God knows who else. We all had one thing in common. We were graduates of the camps. I mean the concentration camps. We were there to train for our trip to Israel. It was kind of a boot camp in a very loose sense.

The instructors were young Israeli men and women. They made us run for miles, march for miles, and fight with knives and sticks, but no weapons. We had two guys in our midst: Palo Hammer and Shlomo Baum. Both took the stick training very seriously. I thought that after all this running and marching we will be introduced to rifles and machine guns. Nothing of the kind. The only handgun I saw was at the initiation into the Hagana on a dark night there in a German forest.

The gals lived in separate quarters but we met in the evenings and had a little fun; mostly singing. One of the gals who joined our group was a blonde with kinky hair, light blue eyes, that looked glazed over, and a forehead like Lenin. She was smart, witty, and spoke many languages, including French. There was a mystique around her; the way she walked, the way she carried herself. She was a year or two older. She was a woman. No wonder I was smitten. From there on I was her companion, nothing serious; a little kissing, a little hugging, or rather a lot of kissing, and a lot of hugging. We spent all our free time together. Was it an interlude or something more? I don't know. I was flattered to be her companion. When we arrived together in Israel, she joined a different kibbutz. I never saw her again!

From Germany, we were transported to the French border, and from there by train for several days, when we arrived at our destination; a cloister somewhere near Marseilles. The military training continued, but now it concentrated more on boarding and abandoning boats. It was soon the day of independence for Israel. Day by day we were alerted to be ready to be shipped out, but the days went by and the routine continued.

May 15, Israel's Independence Day arrived and we were still in France. We could always count on Freddy Karp to come up with something entertaining. Freddy wouldn't let the day go by without something memorable. I don't remember if it was only Freddy, or others who helped him produced a show. There was some singing and dancing. The main attraction was a spoof of Adolf Hitler.

A small table, carried by four brown shirted men, was marched onto the stage. I walked behind the table, dressed in a green jacket, turned back to front, with my hands in the sleeves, ending in a pair of shoes, placed on the table. It created the image of a midget. I was well made up; my hair combed down across my forehead like Adolf. It was eerie! I had a speech prepared, and spoke it as incoherently as Hitler did. I mixed German, Slovak, and Hungarian words, distorted my face, and barked the words to give the impression that the speech was an original, just like the big orator did.

The nuns, priests, and audience of future fighters for the independence of Israel, were rolling in the isles. It was a blast. A few days later we were on our way to Israel!

The departure from France was most dramatic. It was late in the evening when we arrived at a cove on the Mediterranean shore of southern France. The group I belonged to was the first one on the beach. Our instructors were there, running around and giving orders in hushed voices. Slowly, we got used to the darkness. On the horizon, just at the entrance of the cove, we saw something that resembled an anchored ship, rocking on the waves. A projector was set up and signals were sent to it. The ship lifted its anchor and very slowly came toward us. From the forest behind us, we could hear the hum of trucks getting closer and closer. One of the trucks brought a huge package.

In the darkness you couldn't determine the contents. Soon a compressor started to pump air into the strange thing unfolding. It was a rubber landing boat; the one that commandos used in World War II. From the horizon, the ship inched slowly toward the shore.

The ship looked small for a vessel that must plow the open

seas. I knew this was not make believe, this was the real thing. I was sure the small ship would take us to a big one, waiting somewhere beyond the breakers. Was I ever wrong!

The ship dropped its anchor very close to the shore, maybe 150 feet, maybe less. It lowered a small dinghy with oars, a sailor, and what looked like rope. When the dinghy reached us, the rope was secured to a large tree trunk. The rubber boat was then pushed into the water. The rope was secured at both ends. As soon as the rope was secured on the shore, our group was ordered to embark. Once loaded, we pulled on the rope and slowly glided toward the ship. Looking back, I saw trucks packed with people, enter the clearing. They were all the people with whom we spent the last two months.

We climbed a ladder lowered from the ship. On top of the ladder our instructors gave orders as to our positions and tasks for the night. I was sent down to the bottom of the ladder where I was to help the people arriving in the rubber boat. The night was pitch black, the sea, even blacker. I had never seen a sea before, I was a so-so swimmer. I was petrified. However, an order is an order. To ask for relief, I would rather die!

I put one of my free hands around the rope ladder and held on to my belt for dear life. With my free hand, I pulled the arrivals from the rubber boat onto the ladder. The ship was a fishing trawler or small freighter. In the hold were shelves for the arrivals. About 760 men and women were packed like sardines onto those shelves. The shelf designer must have been familiar with the accommodations in the concentration camps, because the similarity was unmistakable. It was eerie!

Not to be bored, Freddy the traffic manager, stood at the top of the ladder, and assigned room numbers to the arrivals. Under the deck, the big boys showed the people to the shelves. They jokingly called the shelves, rooms. After the last man boarded the ship, the rubber boat was pulled onto the deck, deflated and put in storage. Without any fanfare, the ship lifted anchor and we were on our way.

It was early in the morning when the ship, named Fabio, left the cove and entered the Mediterranean Sea. We moved slowly, within sight of the shoreline. It was a calming feeling to know that, in case you had to swim to shore.

Not really! Not me. As I said before, I wasn't much of a

swimmer.

An Italian captained the ship, but we were under the command of an American Jew; probably a Navy man that volunteered for the job. He spoke a little Yiddish with a heavy American accent. His message was clear: We don't know how long we will be on the high seas. We have a limited amount of water or food. Anybody found stealing will be executed. End of statement!

Shlomo Baum was put in charge of executing that order. If Shlomo caught anybody stealing, I don't think there would have been any need for a court martial. Shlomo would have thrown him overboard.

Soon the seas became stormy. The little ship danced on the waves like a match-box. Everybody got sick. Nobody ate. Seemingly, Fero Levy, a member of the group I had befriended, and I, were born sailors, because our appetites increased. The sea became uglier. The ship dipped in every direction. It was frightening. I thought we would never make it. I was cursing Freddy for getting me into this predicament and cursing myself for agreeing.

On the other hand, who knew?

The guys from our group were assigned the day and night watch. We kept watch in the bow of the ship. Laying in the bow of a rocking ship, and a small one to boot, was no pleasure. Because there was no place to sit or stand, we had to lie down on the ropes, and with binoculars, we scanned the horizon. As soon as we saw a ship, no matter how distant, the deck was cleared.

All of us who stood watch, slept on the deck. Only Miki Spiegel had his own quarters. There was a small door in the front of the ship. Behind the door was a small compartment holding the anchor ropes. Miki found enough space there to curl up, and from then on, claimed the hole for himself. One morning I saw him crawling out from his hideout. He wasn't shaven, his hair wasn't combed. He was dirty. I thought for a moment that I saw a mirage. Crawling on all fours, he looked like a small lion.

About the fourth day on the sea, we sailed close to the Italian shore. At midnight, the ship anchored. A small boat approached. The meeting must have been arranged long before. Our instructors were anticipating the meeting. The sea was stormy and the little boat had a hard time to come close. It took hours to secure the lines. The unloading and loading was done in complete secrecy, but on a small ship like ours it was impossible to hide a needle, not to speak of rifles and machine guns.

There were weapons being unloaded from the little boat. Only the instructors were involved. We on the watch, pretended to see nothing.

By the fifth day, the sea calmed. We were still on the open sea. Everybody relaxed, the appetites returned, and nobody gave away his rations anymore. Fero and I spent the rest of the days hungry. The days passed without any excitement. The sailing turned to a routine. I had no idea how long this trip would be, therefore I was no longer concerned. In early morning of the eleventh day, the alarm sounded. A gray ship appeared on the horizon, heading in our direction. The Captain called the troops. The weapons were unpacked; one machine gun, a few rifles, and some submachine guns.

The Captain lined up the fighters on the same side that the gray ship approached, and in a most dramatic manner, announced that we will fight till the last man. We sailed under radio silence; therefore we couldn't find out if the approaching ship was friend or foe. The gray color didn't send an optimistic message. Even so, the gray ship wasn't particularly large. But it looked like a huge sea monster coming to swallow us. It was close enough for us to see the sailors. It was a military ship; a frigate or cruiser.

No rounds were fired. That made us believe that our destiny will be the same as the Exodus and we will end up in Cyprus. To be honest, I thought Cyprus would be more tolerable than to be dead. Moments later, we saw the flag of Israel hoisted up the main mast.

At once, all tension was gone. Laughter and singing took over. The people from deep in the hold ran up to the deck. All 760 of us! We sang Hatikva and Havenu Shalom Aleichem. Then it was back to reality. Back into the hold under the deck. The cruiser shadowed us the whole day. It turned around, only in the evening, but by then we saw the shores of Israel. We felt safe.

Mazel Tov!

We were not surprised when told that we will disembark on the open sea. Nothing could surprise us anymore. Something always happened that we didn't know about or anticipate. Were those young kids; the instructors and their commanders playing dice with our destiny? So it seemed. Or was destiny playing dice with all of us?

The folded rubber boat was hauled out of storage. The compressor started to pump air into the rubber monster that rapidly came alive. Slowly the monster was lowered by ropes into the water. By then we were all lined up and started to jump into the rubber boat. But the rubber boat swung away from the ship. The jump had to be timed precisely so as not to miss the rubber boat. Some guys ended up in the water. The men from the small rowboats that came from the shore as a welcoming party were a magnificent bunch. They dove from their boats before anybody could fall in the sea. They picked us up from the rubber boat and rowed toward the shore. On the shore, people were wading in knee deep water and piggy backed us to the beach. Once on the shore, we fell to our knees and kissed the sand. They were military men; the Hagana or the Palmach, coordinating our arrival. They urged us to stop being sentimental and quickly load up the buses waiting for us. In the morning, I woke up in a military camp. All of us were supposed to be inducted in the newly established army called The Israeli Defense Force. The IDF.

Surprise, surprise! We were not inducted yet. The management of the kibbutz that we were supposed to join was told of our arrival, and before the sun rose we were transferred there. We became soldier-farmers. We worked day time and turned into fighters whenever the sirens blew.

The boot camp was a cruel joke. The man who addressed us introduced himself as Sergeant Joe Doe; clad in military pants and a civilian shirt. He said he is sorry, but all rifles are on the front line and therefore we will have to learn to handle the rifle by imagination. The front line was 200 yards away. After about half an hour of rolling in the dirt, making believe we loaded a rifle, cleaning our hands, and taking the bullets from a belt to load the rifle, we yelled Boom! Boom! Boom! It was hard to decide whose imagination was greater. It was even harder to decide who hit the target and who didn't. After this exercise, we were taken to a makeshift firing range. We were handed Italian carbines with three bullets. If any of the bullets was a dud; it was just tough luck.

It was like firing blanks. All of my three bullets fired. I was ready for the front!

Most of our military involvement was to stand watch. There were only two serious attacks on us in the year and a half we were in the kibbutz. There was intermittent shelling from two cannons stationed in the neighboring Arab village. Some buildings were damaged. A direct hit blew up the water tower, but there were no human casualties from the shelling. There were injuries from sniping; none life threatening. One man was killed during an offensive by a rag-tag group of kibbutzniks.

Two or three stories are worth telling; some outright funny, some lucky, and some close to be considered suicidal.

A group of guys and gals were working in the vegetable garden. It was early in the morning. The vegetable garden was located just outside of the kibbutz fence. The Jordanian Legion, or it might have been the Iraqis that were stationed just beyond the border, started shelling the kibbutz. In cases like this, everybody was ordered to run back to the kibbutz, jump into the nearest trench, and from there continue to your assigned place. One of our gals, who had a slight lisp, ran first; she jumped into the trench and fell. The people running behind her fell on top of her. She started to scream "I am dead; I am dead." Everybody burst out laughing.

I was very lucky the day a shell hit the water tower. Although the tank was made out of steel, it exploded. I was caught running close to the tower, just before the shell hit the tower, I jumped into a very shallow trench. I heard the sound of something hitting the stone in front of me, when I opened my eyes; I. saw a big red piece. I thought my brains were blown out. It took a second to realize I wasn't dead, that it was a piece of steel from the water tower. I got up and ran the fastest I ever did. I might have broken the world record for short distance. I reached the bunker unharmed.

One day the shelling was very heavy. After such a shelling our commanders anticipated a ground assault. Everybody was ordered to stay alert and under no circumstances leave the positions we were supposed to protect. One of the gals, named Ishka Treitel, left her bunker in the middle of the shelling, and went into the kitchen to prepare sandwiches. The dining room wall was hit by a cannon shell where Ishka worked. Not even a cannon shell could shake Ishka's determination to prepare the sandwiches. The crazy part came a little later. When we saw her leaving the kitchen with the sandwiches, and not using the trenches, we started to scream at her to get away from the open space. "The fighters have to eat, and to crawl in the trenches would take a long time," was Ishka's answer. Ishka was 18 years old!

From the beginning, we lived in the children's quarters. The buildings were built of Jerusalem stone. They were bullet proof. The windows facing the enemy were sand bagged; the other side of the house faced the trenches. In case of an alarm, we jumped from the open windows into the trenches, and running through the maze we could reach our assigned positions. I was ready to go to bed, when the alarm sounded. As usual, I jumped out of the window, not realizing that somebody removed the bench that was supposed to be there. I fell and scratched both elbows and knees. That was the only injury I suffered in the five years of living on the border.

On another occasion, I slept so soundly I didn't hear the alarm, nor did I hear the shelling. I didn't arrive at my assigned position. The guys were sure that I was hit on the way to my position. They sent out a searching party but couldn't find me. When the all clear sounded and every body returned to the quarters, I was still floating on cloud number nine. They thought that I was hit in my bed and was dead. Nobody ever believed that I didn't hear the alarm, not to speak of the shelling.

Life soon turned into a routine. I was assigned to work in the orchards. As nature always does what nature wants, my stint in the orchard didn't last too long. A Polish group arrived that was supposed to join the kibbutz as members, so I, as a temporary, was sent to work in the garden, not to learn the trade, just to do odd jobs. We already had two guys that were supposed to be the gardeners. Our management didn't object because by then it was decided that we would not grow an orchard. I was a good guy and said nothing. I was a good worker. I would chase the mules, plowing without mercy. The manager of the garden told me to slow down; he was concerned about the mules. He didn't feel any sympathy for me.

A short time after I started to work in the garden, two new groups arrived at the kibbutz. Both groups were scheduled to become members. We were transporting irrigation pipe from section to section. Four men were assigned to the job. The Polish kid made some stupid error, opening a connection that could have snapped the pipe. I must have said something that wasn't to his liking. He was an arrogant little bastard. I didn't react. We finished one part and went to see Kostia, a member of our group, who was in charge of irrigation, to get further instructions. I told Kostia about the exchange I had with the kid. I spoke Slovak. I didn't realize that Yoel, the kid's name, understood what I was saying. He again opened his big mouth and was coming at me. I thought he was going to hit me. Just to be sure I clocked him first. He went down like a sack of potatoes. I was a little concerned because he was lying there, hardly moving. Then he opened his eyes. I was standing on top of him, when he asked for more. I told him to get up so I could clock him again. He didn't.

In the kibbutz it was unacceptable to use physical force. The rule was more sacred than the Ten Commandments. Fist fights? Not in a kibbutz! But it happened. I knew I made a terrible mistake, but it was too late to apologize. Yoel was on his way to the manager of the garden to file a complaint. The manager came toward us with his head bent, not looking at us. I knew what's coming. He had to fire me. He had no choice. It didn't matter that the work was interrupted. I was sent home.

Because I wasn't under the jurisdiction of Kibbutz Maanit, the matter was transferred to our group. The two managers came to an agreement. I would accept a punishment; to work for three months in the kitchen, or to leave the kibbutz. I went to work in the kitchen.

After my stint in the kitchen, I was sent back to work in the vegetable garden. I was sent to a shed where the potatoes, imported from the Netherlands, were disinfected and sorted. The potatoes came in hundred pound crates. My work, together with my friend, Dov Steckel, was to submerge the crates in the disinfecting liquid, then pull the crate out and take it to the shed where the old-timers and our gals did the sorting. One of the old timers, Shosha, told us that for the two minutes while we waited for the potatoes being submerged, we should join them to sort, instead of loafing and smoking cigarettes. I told her that the work is very hard. To lift hundred pound crates soaked with liquid, every two minutes, was equal to slavery. If there had been any consideration on the part of the kibbutz they would have brought in more people and given us an hour off for every two hours of work. I could have stopped there. But I didn't. I continued.

Every two minutes I came up with a new list of mistreatments accusing the management of the kibbutz. First, we were supposed to learn trades, but most of us worked as Negro laborers, shuffled from place to place. After a year in the kibbutz we were masters of everything and knew nothing. I told old timer Shosha, that I was ready to forgive the management's behavior under the duress of the war, but the war was long over and our fortunes didn't change. Shosha got red in her face.

I knew I had hit a sensitive spot. She got angrier by the minute, and I pushed for the kill. I had hundreds of complaints, but the big one was just generating in my little brain. I told her that we were supposed to work only five days. One day every week we were supposed to get instructions in Hebrew. I told her that I don't want to be petty, but our group consists of 100 men and women. They owe us 5,600 hours of overtime for one year. I knew that we were not worth that much, so I was ready to make a deal. Kibbutz Maanit just received a tractor. It was a tractor on rubber wheels, made by McCormack, with the blazing red color. Brand new! So I told Shosha that as payment for the days we worked instead of learning, we will take the tractor with us when we leave to build our own settlement. I threw the bomb, and it exploded with more force than I dreamed of. Actually I thought about the whole episode as a joke. Shosha didn't. She wasn't too concerned about my complaints. She became incensed about the tractor. She blew her top and ran to the secretary of Kibbutz Maanit to file a complaint against me. As I mentioned before, Kibbutz Maanit had no jurisdiction over me. All matters had to be brought before our assembly. The secretary of Maanit requested that I should appear in front of Maanit's assembly and retract all my accusations and apologize.

Fat chance! They got the wrong guy to back down.

The secretary of our group didn't give in either. The old timers were furious. Every time I passed by one of them, I got the evil eye. I couldn't care less. Truthfully, I enjoyed the comedy.

The secretary of Kibbutz Maanit was flabbergasted. He couldn't let the matter remain unresolved. The ideology of our communal society called for fairness, but what they did was less than fair. At the end, I accused the kibbutz of being amoral and not living up to the standards that our ideology called for. They felt caught red handed.

I had them cornered. And I wasn't going to let up. Every day I came up with new demands. I became a pest. Some of our guys were not too happy about me carrying on. Oh, how hard it is to swallow the truth!

Our guys named the tractor Chaviva. Chaviva Reich was a paratrooper in World War II; dropped behind German lines, she was captured, and executed. In her honor, our group was named Lhavot Chaviva (the Flames of Chaviva). To the old timers, to name the tractor Chaviva, was like pouring salt into an open wound. Two months after the affair, we left Kibbutz Maanit to build our own settlement. The tractor remained in Maanit to remind the old timers of the pest who demanded fairness, morality, and ethics.

We got our own Red Tractor and a yellow Caterpillar, to boot.

THE TWO LOVE AFFAIRS

After one or two small loves, and a year in the kibbutz, my big love, Katka Frankova, left. She wanted to return the rings I had given her. That's how big this love was. I took back the ring that I inherited from my father, but my grandmother's tiny diamond, I insisted she keep. I cried when she left. I thought I would never see her again. I was heartbroken. It wasn't the first time, and not the last time either. Well, I didn't see her for a long time. I was 20 years old, something had to happen.

It did.

A group of Slovak kids joined the kibbutz. They were supposed to become members as soon as they reached the ripe age of 18. The girls and boys were teenagers. Most were 15 years old, but some were even younger.

Saturday evening's dances were held in the dining room. The tables were pushed to the wall. The middle became the dance floor. The local talent played mostly horas and Israeli folk dances, but once in a while a tango or waltz was inserted in the program. I liked to dance and was on the floor all the time. When the tune was a waltz, very few couples took the opportunity to show off their versatility. The young girls lined up against the wall. One little blonde, with kinky hair, swayed to the music. I figured she must know how to dance. I crossed the room and asked her to waltz. She was a good dancer; cute, but just another kid. The next time a waltz was played I assumed that we would dance together. Her name was Lia, but I named her Valtshik, the Slovak word for waltz.

We soon started to date. It was "verboten" (forbidden) for the youngsters to date the older guys. We are the old guys? Hardly twenty. There were a few reasons why the kibbutz tried to keep us apart. First, they were afraid we would convince the girls to join our group. The second reason was more legitimate. They were concerned that the young girls might get involved in relationships that will be more than kissing and hugging.

160

Nevertheless, relationships did develop; one was ours; Lia and me. It wasn't easy. Lia worked in the tree nursery and one of our gals worked in the same place. I used her to convey messages to Lia. This tryst had to be kept most secret. The danger was that Lia could have been thrown out of the kibbutz, and I had nothing else to offer her. On the other hand, when we saw each other, I had to be very careful not to create a situation where her life would become stressful. I was amazed at how well she handled the situation. She was only 15 years old.

We had a great time together. Lia decided to introduce me to her family. First we traveled to Kibbutz Haogen, where her sister lived. I wasn't too comfortable in her sister's presence, and even less with her husband. What the hell were they thinking? They must have questioned Lia about details. Such as do you have sex with this old man? When she told them the truth, they probably didn't believe her. I don't blame them. On the other hand, the decision to have an intimate relationship was ours. I guess it was more mine than Lia's. From Haogen we traveled to Natanya, where her parents lived. Lia must have prepared them before we came to visit. I felt more comfortable in their house. They must have concluded that I am a responsible young man. I hardly recall how we returned to the kibbutz. I remember that I let her go first, and I lingered on the road until I saw that she reached the gate of the kibbutz. I took the back road so as not to be spotted.

At the conclusion of my antics in Kibbutz Maanit, I paid a heavy price. The secretary of Maanit found a way out of his dilemma. At that time, the headquarters of our organization decided to send one man from each kibbutz to help rebuild Kibbutz Negba that had been ravaged in the war of 1948. Who was a better candidate than me? With one swat, the secretary of Maanit killed two flies. He separated me from Lia (by then everybody knew that we were an item) and got rid of a pest who came up with new demands every day.

My stint in Kibbutz Negba turned out to be an adventure. The guy I shared a room with was from the neighboring kibbutz. He asked me about my profession. I told him that I am a truck driver. "They would never let you drive one of their brand new trucks. Tell them you are a painter." He said.

"Are you crazy? I never held a brush in my hand." I replied.

"Do not worry," he told me. "I will teach you."

So I became a painter. I missed Lia but I had no way to get in touch with her without further complicating her life. My partner left, and I was the painter who was a truck driver, who had no idea what he was doing. All the new buildings were painted white, so it was easy to satisfy my client.

THE RAINS

At the end of my stint in Negba, I went to the new settlement, Gazie, which my friend had started just a few days before. I couldn't imagine how anxious one member was to have me back. Micki Spiegel was the builder; the contractor. The first morning on the job Micki and I went to the empty lot where a chicken coop was to be built. Micki was measuring by pulling small strings, acting like an engineer.

I was impressed!

Micki told me that as soon as he finished with the measurements we would start building the base for the chicken coop. Since the shed was only a temporary structure, few thoughts were given to its longevity. He told me to build a wall around the shed using the concrete blocks that were piled up next to the lot. I assumed my job was to hand Micki the blocks and cement, and he will build the wall. He mixed the cement and left.

"Hey, where are you going?"

Oh, he is busy some other place, was his answer. I told him that I never did anything similar, not to speak of building a wall. Micki told me it isn't a big deal, the cement was already mixed and all I had to do was follow the strings he prepared. He left. I started to lay down the first row of blocks and found that Micki was right. You didn't have to be a rocket scientist to build a wall. Usually I work fast, so building this wall wouldn't be any different. By the time I had the third row finished, I looked up and saw that the wall had a bulge leaning to the outside. Micki came back to check on my progress. I mentioned the bulge and told him that the two rows should be rebuilt. He said, "Oh, don't worry, when we put down the two by fours it will make no difference."

In the middle of the night on the day we brought the first 5,000 baby chicks, a very strong wind toppled the shed. All 5,000 chicks took off toward the Jordanian border. We chased the little yellow things all night. Next day the shed was returned to its place. So the bulge in the base did make a difference!

For the first six months, we stayed in Jelemi. It was located west of Gazie, where our permanent settlement was to be built. I don't remember the reason, but it made some sense. Gazie was close to the border and a fence had to be erected before we could bring in the children that were popping up, one after the other, like the baby chicks. So far we had three children, with two more on the way. In Jelemi, we erected two wooden trailer-like structures; a dining room with a kitchen attached, and large military tents.

In the beginning, we were only 20 to 30 members living in Jelemi. To make a living, most of our guys and gals worked in the neighboring villages and returned home Friday. The rainy season started early that year. The hill that we were on was red clay, but the surrounding fields were black soil. When it rained, the fields surrounding the hill got so muddy we didn't dare venture beyond the red clay.

For one of those weeks we were completely cut off. The telephone didn't work, nor did the emergency radio. We ran short of food and the bread supply dwindled. It was decided that one of us would attempt to cross the fields and bring help. Because I was the only horseman in the bunch, it became my duty to carry out the rescue.

We had two mules. I saddled the stronger one and was on my way. The mule sank in the mud, but we made good progress. I was sure I would succeed in the mission. Only the wadi separated us, (me and my mule), from reaching the road. Due to the heavy rains, the normally dry riverbed (wadi) was flooded. Horses know how to swim. I wasn't sure about the mules. I got off the mule. I had on knee high rubber boots. I tried to see if I could reach bottom.

I didn't!

I mounted the mule and urged her to cross the river. The stupid mule did the same thing as I. When she didn't feel the bottom, she turned around and wouldn't enter the river

I tried every trick I knew. Nothing worked!

The mule wasn't so stupid, after all. I was livid. I was ready to kill her. If I had a gun in my pocket I would have knocked her off right there. But what could I do? I could never cross the muddy fields. To return without bringing help would be too embarrassing. The mule made the final decision. She turned around and headed home.

By Friday, the water had receded and our dirt road looked passable. David drove the Caterpillar tractor to pick up the guys and gals that arrived by truck to the edge of the wadi. Scanning the clay road with binoculars, we saw our group, including David, wading with packages on their backs. David said the tractor got stuck not far from the kibbutz. He asked us to bring the rubber wheeled red McCormack tractor to pull him out. We took chains and cables, mounted the rubber wheeled tractor and went to his rescue.

At the spot where David claimed the tractor got stuck we saw no tractor. It couldn't have been stolen. We figured the guys decided to play a joke on us. About 100 yards away there was an abandoned building. We figured that maybe they hid the tractor there. We looked, but saw no tractor. All of a sudden, someone saw a tractor exhaust pipe sticking out of the mud. A group of us worked four days to clear the mud around the sunken tractor. And then we still had to borrow the largest Caterpillar tractor available, to pull our smaller one from the mud. David was exonerated!

Once in about 60 years, Israel gets a snowfall in the middle of the country. It had to happen to us. A foot of snow fell overnight. The tents collapsed. We spent the remainder of the night sleeping in the dining room. By 10 in the morning the warm sun had melted all the snow. The only reminder of the snow was the tents lying in the mud.

The two couples that came to visit us chose a most difficult time to do so. They were stuck with us for a few days. But by the end of the week they decided to cross the muddy fields. They tried to reach the railroad tracks that were about half a mile west of our kibbutz. We tried to convince them to wait another day, to no avail.

An hour later, we saw people in the muddy field. But we were not sure who they were. Somebody was smart enough to grab the binoculars and check out the situation. Everyone from the kibbutz came to see the show. The four visitors were stuck in the mud. As soon as one was pulled out, another one sunk. They began to get desperate, but they were too far away for us to hear their calls for help.

As soon as we realized the danger, a rescue party was organized. We took wooden planks and ropes. One by one, we pulled the four to safe ground. They left the next day, together with our workers, via the Caterpillar tractor.

The rainy season came to an end. Spring was only a few days

away. The mud turned into black soil again. The dirt road was passable, and the wadi was dry. The time had come to move forward; to start building our permanent kibbutz on the hill of Gazie that from then on would be called "Kibbutz L'havot Haviva."

BUILDING A NEW KIBBUTZ

The first task was to erect the fence. There was a water hole on the premises, but we weren't sure whether the water was safe to drink. The place turned into a beehive. The empty hill began to take shape as a functioning village.

The place buzzed all day with the noise of motors and humans running up and down. Toward evening everything calmed; the members returned to Jelemi for the night. On the hill, only a small contingency of watchmen remained. In reality, they were soldiers for the night.

We erected housing for the members; a large structure for the dining room, and the kitchen that could accommodate a hundred people at the same time. The next task was to build the permanent housing for 20,000 chickens, a shed for 60 cows, and so on; everything that a farm needs.

When everything was in place, we realized that we would not be able to make a living from the land. Therefore, we bought three trucks and joined a trucking cooperative. Dov was the senior truck driver, with Michael second in command. They drove ten-ton Mack diesels, I got the new truck; a five-ton International Harvester. My experience was limited.

I was learning on the job!

One morning I passed a truck unloading workers. One of the workers, an older man, appeared to be in a hurry and couldn't wait until all the others got off on the right side of the road. He decided to step off on the left. As I passed the truck, his backpack got caught on one of the hooks on my truck and he was pulled between the two trucks.

I was devastated!

An ambulance took the man to the nearest hospital. There were no police involved and no report was filed. I couldn't sleep for nights. I had nightmares. There was nobody to complain to. We had no psychiatrist on the premises. I continued driving, but with a lot more caution.

The old man, who looked old to me; maybe 45, disappeared.

167

He never returned to work at the kibbutz I did trucking for. Nevertheless, every time I passed the place, I was reminded of the accident.

About a year later, I was summoned to appear in court in Natanya. I had no idea that the accident would end up in court. The lawyer for my insurance company was there. We had a 15 minute meeting before the judge appeared. My lawyer put me on the witness stand and let me describe the situation to the best of my knowledge.

Did I remember? "Every second of it! I lived with this nightmare for a whole year." That's what I said. The old man's lawyer declined to cross-examine. The judge threw the case out. I thought that was the end of it.

Half a year later, I was summoned to a court in Tel-Aviv. Again I was put on the stand. The court bailiff asked me to swear on the bible. Because I belonged to a kibbutz where all members were atheists, I was afraid the judge would question the conflict of interest involved. Therefore, I turned to the judge and told him that I can't swear on the bible because I am non-believer. The judge bent over his bench and asked me, "What don't you believe in, young man?" I had no choice! He put me on the spot! I looked straight into his eyes, and said, "I don't believe in God." I knew I had to stare down the judge. It wasn't easy. He was a man in his sixties; distinguished. His hair; silver gray, and a round face with rosy cheeks.

And who was I? A twenty year old "kaker!" (shitter).

It was one of the most difficult times in my young life. The old man claimed that he would be incapacitated all his life because of the accident, but when called to the stand, he ran up the stairs. He forgot that he was supposed to limp. There was laughter in the court.

I won the case!

The trucking was a successful enterprise. We searched for more business. There was another kibbutz in the neighborhood that belonged to the same organization as we did. They had a food factory. Actually the food production was limited to orange and lemon juices, pickles, and jams. With the help of the headquarters of our common organization, it was decided to merge us into the factory. It was agreed that we will send eight men to work in the factory, and after a trial period we would become a minority owner. What our share was,

I don't remember. It was really unimportant. I'm sure that if the arrangement came to fruition it would have been a fair deal.

Two men from our kibbutz were supposed to be on the board of directors. All together, eight men from our kibbutz had to work in the factory, and two had to serve on the board of directors. The nominating committee suggested that Dan Mayer and I should serve on the board. Dan was nominated, but the secretary of the kibbutz challenged my nomination. He claimed that if I worked in any division of the kibbutz, it would be a conflict of interest; my interest would be solely for the division, and not for the kibbutz.

Is the success of a division detrimental to the company that fully owns it? Only politicians can come up with such nonsense. True, the secretary wasn't a rocket scientist, and I strongly believe that somebody else was responsible for the challenge of my nomination, and the secretary just went along with it. On the other hand, they did me a favor. I never wanted to be in a position where I had to use my power, to force things down somebody's throat.

I didn't fight for the job. I thought politics doesn't belong in the life style we chose.

Was I ever wrong!

From the first day in the factory, all eight of us were assigned to the production line of filling bottles with orange juice. I asked the manager how many bottles a day were produced by the crew we replaced. I was shocked to hear that only 2,000 bottles came off the line in an eight-hour shift. It made no sense to produce so few. My next question was what is the market price for a bottle of orange juice? The manager wouldn't answer my question. "Just do your job and we will take care of the rest," was his reply. That's all I had to hear. My relationship with the manager started off on the left foot and never changed.

All the work was manual. Ruven, one of the eight from our kibbutz, and I, were in charge of capping the bottles. We saw that the snag was at the capping position, and if that problem could be solved, we could produce many more. The caps for the bottles were imported from the USA. We learned that some of the caps were made of steel and some of aluminum. We started to use only the aluminum caps and in no time we produced more than 10,000 bottles a day.

Our success didn't sit well with the manager. Every time he

passed by, I asked for his approval for a job well done. This drove him crazy. I was dismissed from the factory and became a truck driver again.

I wonder who was behind the decision to dismiss me. If they thought I was the cause of the problem, that was not so. The partnership never came to fruition. Mermelstein, the manager of Kibbutz Gan-Shmuel, made sure to undermine our success, and I wouldn't be surprised if the rest of the management had a hand in it too. Yes, I was a pest, but a positive one.

I was an ant, not a cockroach!

For the second anniversary celebration of our existence as an independent kibbutz, we decided to put on a show; a drama. The work of a Russian writer was chosen. A simple story. An American soldier with the rank of captain, and his wife, are serving in Germany after World War II. They realize the injustices of the American society and both turn Communist. The play was sanctioned by all the committees involved in planning the celebration.

I was considered to be some kind of a local talent. I got the leading part as Captain Kidd and Ruth Neuman played Cynthia, my wife. The direction was entrusted to a veteran director from Kibbutz Ein Shemer.

Notwithstanding the fact that the whole production, the scenery, and the uniforms were shabby and amateurish, the show was a big success! So much so, the politicos of our organization decided to take the show on the road. The first performance was supposed to open in Jerusalem. The show was scheduled to open at eight in the evening. Seemingly the authorities got wind of the anti American rhetoric. Minutes before the opening, the police, I don't remember under what pretense, closed the theater. The show never opened!

I could have been a contender!

I could have been somebody!

Dov Tesler and I continued studying under the Slovak Film director, Ladislav Lahola. But to our chagrin, he moved to the USA, and the drama circle was dissolved. I continued to dabble in staging shows. I was the producer, director, and sometimes the actor, too. Nothing serious; amateurish stuff. I wasn't an acting-between-jobs waiter, I was a truck driver!

I destroyed the KB7 truck that I drove. Instead of five tons I would load seven, or even eight tons. Something had to give. The truck did. I was transferred to the Mack Diesel crew. I was a skinny little guy, hardly 110 pounds; maybe 115. The big truck did a job on me. It avenged the destruction of the KB7. My back hurt badly, and it came to a point where I had to concede defeat.

Now that I was idle, I had to find a job where my back could recuperate. I took a course in treating manure. The gentleman who gave the course made us feel good by telling us that the job is a very important one. He, with his expertise in the science of manure, was able to visit the whole world. I wasn't satisfied with either his description or promises to travel the world. I wanted a diploma with a rubber stamp and a title. There were no diplomas and no titles at the end of a week long course.

It reminded me of a childhood game we played in Zdana, the village where I was born. First we asked some difficult questions, like how far is the earth from the sun, from the moon, from the stars. Nobody had an answer. Then we turned to questions about the shape and color of animal waste. The answers in every case got an A+. So we said to the kid, "About science you have no idea, but about shit, you know everything." My test at the end of the course fetched an A+. No wonder. I was an expert from a long time ago. I had extensive knowledge of the subject from Auschwitz.

I thought I should give dignity to the job. I gave myself a title "Shit Master General." I didn't ask the kibbutz to put a rubber stamp on the document. I was content with the title.

In 1953 I got very sick. I contracted typhoid. My fever was sky high. The doctor who saw me twice a week, decided that I have a bad cold, and prescribed aspirin, three times a day. The high fever didn't lower. Actually it went higher as the days went by. I was very weak. I couldn't eat. The only thing I could swallow was warm milk. By the eighth day I asked the substitute nurse to call for an ambulance. The ambulance took me to Rambam hospital in Haifa. The nurse took my temperature, but I had none. The doctor who came to see me was told about my condition and about the fact that I am free of fever. He lifted my shirt and said it was typhoid that just broke. He prescribed rest and good food and told the ambulance driver to take me home. I lost a lot of weight. I had very little to lose to start with. I looked terrible and my mother was soon coming to visit. She hadn't seen me for more than five years.

MY MOTHER'S FIRST VISIT TO ISRAEL

When I had taken my mother to Prague, on her way to the USA, she was 45 years old. But she looked much older. She was devastated and looked it. And why not? She had lost her husband and a child, not to speak of the rest of her family. The wounds were too fresh; it was less than two years since the end of the war. The uncertainty about the future showed in her face.

Now, more than eight years later, a ravishing, young, 54 year old walked off the ramp. For a moment I thought I saw a mirage, I hardly recognized her. She was well dressed, confident, with a spring in her walk. She arrived with her husband, Martin, who had family in Haifa and hadn't seen any of them in more than 30 years. Martin immigrated to the USA in the late twenties and was a veteran of World War II. He had volunteered and was in the second wave at Omaha Beach.

We were not paid in the kibbutz. We were given credit for overtime above the required weekly 54 hours. With the accumulated hours we could take a prolonged vacation. I had accumulated 540 overtime hours. I took five weeks off and joined my parents. They rented a car, and we started to travel. First, came the visits to relatives. Martin had a mother, sisters, and brothers, scattered over Israel. After finishing the visiting rounds, we traveled to the north.

We stopped in Tiberias and checked into the best hotel. The hotel had a restaurant. As soon as we set down, Martin took over. He ordered a steak for four and explained to the waiter exactly how the streak should be prepared. The waiter listened patiently. Then he said, "I am sorry sir, but I can't serve meat to the Israelis." Martin became incensed. He threw a shit fit. He called the manager: I was so ashamed. I was ready to run from the restaurant. I tried to explain to him that it is perfectly all right for me to order a pasta dish. It is the law of Israel, and we respect it.

The manager was smarter. He told Martin to order a big steak.

He could then eat it or share it with me. Then the steak came. In those times all meat was imported from Argentina and only God knows how many times the damn stuff was defrosted and refrozen. The steak wasn't medium rare, it was well done. It was gray. Martin became the ugly, arrogant American. He carried on like a mad man. My mother didn't like what she saw.

At that moment, it occurred to me that destiny had been good to me. Going to Israel instead of the USA was a blessing.

At every opportunity, she tried to talk me into leaving the kibbutz and come to the USA. She had no idea about the political situation we were a part of. I was a member of a socialist party; an active member to boot. She didn't know that the US government restricted the visitation of subversive elements. And I, as a member of a socialist party, that considered Stalin a revisionist, surely belonged to that subversive element. The chances of me getting a visitors visa were as far fetched as man walking on the moon. In 1953 I did not have a vision of President Kennedy.

Nevertheless I promised that I would apply.

As usual, in situations like this, entanglements are the rule. First I had to apply to the kibbutz for a prolonged vacation. In cases like this, the matter had to be brought in front of the full assembly of the kibbutz, where a simple majority could decide whether the vacation should be granted or not. There was no objection from the floor. I was free to apply for a visa to the USA.

THE ROAD BUILDER

As soon as my parents left for their home in the US, I was given a new job. Whoever chose me for the job had no idea what was at stake. The government had allocated money to build a paved road from Ein Shemer Airport -- a military facility erected by the American and British Army, and not in use -- to our kibbutz. The contractor asked the kibbutz to send a man to build the road. Nobody knew why the contractor wanted a kibbutznik to be on the road job. I was told to meet the road engineer, who would enlighten me about my job. The engineer spoke only Rumanian and broken Hebrew, and didn't know why I was sent to work on the road. The workers who unloaded sand from trucks, all spoke Arabic. They were Jews from Algeria or Tunisia, and maybe some from Morocco. There were also those that unloaded stones from a truck. They spoke Kurdish. Tower of Babel? You got it!

Around noontime, a jeep pulled up to the road and asked for the man from the kibbutz. I recognized the guy. He was the manager of the roads between Hedera and TelAviv. I knew him from when I hauled stones to the roads there. Kuba was his name. He found me unloading a truck with stones and greeted me. "What the hell are you doing unloading stones? I have enough workers. I need a manager."

I joined Kuba in his jeep and off we went. "Kuba, what are you talking about? Are you crazy? I have no idea about road building."

"You did a lot of hauling materials to the roads. You saw enough. The work won't be completely strange to you."

"If you say so Kuba. So be it."

"Do not worry. I will teach you everything you have to know."

He reminded me of Mr. Nrets, the White Gorilla who taught me bookkeeping. Now I am going to get a crash course in road building.

Mazel Tov!

In his office, Kuba pulled out the blue prints for the road. "Here you put twenty centimeters of sand. Then you top it with twenty centimeters of stone and that's all for building a road. The road is about three kilometers long, with two small and one large bridge. The engineer is there. If you have any questions, come to my office."

Three hours of a crash course and I was elevated to the rank of manager.

Mazel Tov. Today I am a road builder!

I hoped for a jeep. I got a horse; a white one. I wondered why I wasn't given an ass!

The second day on the job, feeling very important, I rode on my white horse for the length of the road, to review the troops. I felt like General Patton. One didn't have to be a rocket scientist to realize the sorry state of the enterprise. I knew that the road had to be finished before the rainy season. The Kurds were diligent workers, but the African contingency was a complete disaster. I asked Kuba for permission to hire more Kurd workers. Kuba had no objections. Just the opposite, he was very attentive to my request. The more Kurds I hired, the more Africans I had to fire. I didn't realize that I had stepped into a hornet's nest.

Politics!

The African Jews belonged to the same political party as our kibbutz. Namely the Socialists. The Kurds were from the opposition Social Democratic party. This didn't set well with the guys from the union. They called for a meeting. The meeting was held in the offices of our kibbutz with four guys from the union, the kibbutz manager, and me.

Without any formalities, I was told by the union guys to stop hiring and firing people. The union didn't hire me, so I didn't feel obligated to grant their demands. At the meeting, I turned to our secretary, and asked him point blank, "Do you want the road finished before the rainy season or not? Because the workers I fired wouldn't be able to build the road in ten years not to speak of six months."

Our secretary told me that he couldn't make a decision without discussing it with all members of the secretariat.

I got very angry. I was sure our secretary would take my side without hesitation. Being hot tempered, I was surprised that I didn't quit the job on the spot. On the other hand, I believed that my decision was right and that I handled the situation according to the necessities. I had no other agenda but to have the road done on time. I don't think well when angry. I had to calm down. I had to find a way to circumvent the politicians.

I came up with a brilliant idea.

The workers that I had were satisfactory for unloading the truck but to build a road I needed men that had the know-how. There was an airfield next to us. I figured that the men who built the runways must be from the neighborhood. If they know how to build a runway, they would be able to build a road. I asked for permission to investigate.

I found that the men who built the runways live in the neighboring Arab village of Baka-el-Garbhie. I approached our secretary and told him about my findings. I also told him that he has to make a decision without further delays. To my surprise, I got the green light. I could hire 60 men from the Arab village. I was also told to get in touch with Ahmed, who was hired as the night watchman for the road. He will give me a list of people who belong to our political party. This way we got all the politicians off our back.

At the time, the Arab village was under military administration. Permits were given to men only after a background check. I met the commanding officer in his office in Baka-el-Garbhie and presented him with my request. He told me, very politely, that he has nothing to do with my request. I must present it to the local mayor. If the mayor agrees, I would have to bring the names to him for a security check. The mayor was as friendly as can be. He hardly looked at the list. He signed the request and also invited me to a sumptuous dinner.

Two days later, I had 60 Arab men working on the road. And work they did! I retained some of the Jewish workers; mostly the Kurds. With all the groups coordinated in one continuous operation, the road started to take shape. I rode my horse back and forth, and watched the progress, like a proud father seeing his child grow.

The only unpleasantness occurred when I was asked to sign receipts for sand and stones delivered to the kibbutz instead of to the road.

I refused!

For my refusal to sign bogus receipts, I was called every name in the book; for being disloyal to the kibbutz, and for being hardheaded. Some even went so far as to call me a "Chamnor" (ass). But the biggest compliment I received was given by my friends who

177

called me an idiot.

It didn't matter. I was sure that my refusal to cheat was correct.

An engineer from Tel-Aviv came to examine the road and the bridges. Kuba never showed up. The workers and the Rumanian engineer were gone. I was the only one left to accompany the distinguished visitor from Tel-Aviv. We started to walk from the runways toward the kibbutz. I brought the blue prints with me. He appeared satisfied with the results. He examined the two small bridges and the large one that was very close to the end of the road. The blue prints called for 20 centimeters of sand under the base of the bridge. According to the engineer, it had to be 200 centimeters. "Oh my God, this bridge won't survive the first winter," was his reaction.

Was he wrong!

The road ended at the entrance to the kibbutz. I convinced the secretary of the kibbutz to continue the road into the kibbutz so the trucks could be parked inside the fence. My plan was accepted with the condition that I build the road and will receive help only if people are available. I accepted the challenge. Micki Spiegel volunteered to do the measurements and also hammered the stakes for the 150 meter long road. From there on, it became my baby. Once in a while, Zvi Joseph and Ruven Newman came to help, but most of the time I worked alone. The road was finished before the rainy season. When the first truck rolled up the hill, on my road, I was on cloud nine. However, I got no acknowledgement from the cheverim or the kibbutz management, or as much as a tap on the shoulder.

I didn't give a flying f---. So why do I write about it now?

Go figure!

As much as I was concerned, those were the most exhilarating days of my five year stint in the kibbutz. I loved every minute of it.

Why do good things end too fast and bad ones linger on forever?

Ahmed, the watchman, continued to remain on the road until all the equipment was removed. I visited him occasionally. I was invited to his house for elegant dinners served by his three or four wives. Under some weird circumstances, I found that the list of workers that Ahmed supplied did not include the names of members of our political party, but were all relatives of the mayor. I had 60 relatives of the mayor working on my road. I confronted Ahmed with my findings. He was very apologetic. He said he had no choice. He said that he knew the job was only temporary and that eventually he would have to return to the village. If he had followed my request, he would have been ostracized for life in the village. I wrote off the whole matter.

Now I was unemployed. I could have got my truck driver's job back because Itzig Katz, who replaced me, was leaving the kibbutz with his wife, Chana. So did Avri and Bela Shuli, and Klari Zalman, my dear friend, and many more. I had no plans to leave. I liked the kibbutz life in spite of the shortcomings. I liked the fairness of the system, not perfect, but fairer than anything else I had experienced before or after.

I had permission to apply for a visa to visit my parents. I did not apply. I knew that the chances of getting a visa were nil. I was a card-carrying member of the Socialist Party. It was McCarthy times in the US. No commies, no pinkos, and no reds were allowed to enter, and I was more than red. I was burgundy!

THE INQUISITION

I was summoned to a meeting with the secretary of the kibbutz. When I entered the room, I found all nine members of the secretariat were there. I realized that something very important would be discussed. I thought that I will be asked to join the Mossad (Secret Service) or maybe something even more important.

The secretary opened the meeting. He elaborated on the importance of the meeting being held; therefore all members of the secretariat were asked to attend.

OK. So what is the beef?

In one word, the secretariat asked me to rescind my application to visit the USA. I don't like to be bullied and at the moment I felt I was. I am surprised how calm I was.

The secretary told me that he learned that I planned to leave the kibbutz and immigrate to the USA. I said his assumption was ridiculous. I hadn't even applied for the visa, and since I am a card-carrying member of the Socialist party, the chances of me getting one were close to zero. I must have pushed the right button, because he said he could prove I was lying. They have a letter from my mother saying I shouldn't be afraid to come to the States; that everything would be taken care of. I started to laugh. For the past five years I received letters like this. "Did I leave the kibbutz?" I asked. "Anyway, how did you get my mother's letter? Are you opening my mail?"

"No," he said, "somebody found it in a book you returned to the library."

"And on this you are basing the accusation and calling me a liar?" I asked.

I told the assembled dignitaries that they have no right to change the decision that was made by the full assembly of the kibbutz. The secretary was adamant. He threatened me with expulsion. I told him that according to the kibbutz rules, he must bring the matter in front of the assembly. If the assembly decides that the vacation permit should be withdrawn, then, so be it. The secretary didn't agree with my request.

180

I played the game.

My mind was made up. I was going to leave the kibbutz, no matter what. And I wasn't leaving alone. I was leaving with my wife, Anita. I kept my mouth shut; most unusual for me. I told the group that I would be back the next evening with my answer.

The next morning, Anita and I took the day off and traveled to Haifa. Before my mother had left Israel to return to the States, she told me that if I had any problems, I should ask my stepfather's sister for help. I met Ella and her husband. I told them of my decision to leave the kibbutz. They were very gracious. I had no idea that my parents foresaw my problems of leaving the kibbutz.

We returned the same day to the kibbutz. I met the secretary. I told him that his request was unacceptable. We decided to leave the kibbutz. At the same time, I asked him to call a special meeting of all the membership of the kibbutz, where we would announce our departure.

At these meetings, every member had the right to be heard. For every practical purpose, it was a put down session. The members who liked me were quiet. The ones who didn't, could spill all the venom they felt. They had a hard time defacing me; I was a good worker, and a loyal member of the political party to which we belonged. I was the only one who had given up his leather jacket; the birthday gift I got from my mother. I turned the jacket in for the common use. Nobody else did! I had no problems with sharing. Sharing was what I liked! In many forms.

The session couldn't end without a reprimand. In every group there must be a smart ass, and our kibbutz had plenty. I remember the smart ass member. I won't mention his name. He was one of the brightest in the group. He came up with a line that rings in my ears to this day. His parting lines were: "You lived here like an actor and now you are leaving like a comedian."

Little did he know how right he was!

The kibbutz supplied us with a small truck to carry our meager belongings and us to Haifa. At the end of the dirt road, across from Kibbutz Gan-Shmuel, the truck refused to continue. I mean the engine quit. I went to the factory where I had worked and asked for permission to make a phone call. The Hadera trucking company agreed to give us a lift for 13 Lira. That's all the money we had!

In Haifa, I applied for a visitor's visa to the USA. The

interview with the officer in the USA consulate ended in a disaster. The interviewing officer was nasty. I had no idea what provoked his anger. He asked me if I belong to the Communist party. I told him that I was a member of the Socialist-Zionist party Mapam. The policy of Mapam was against the Communist party; because they were anti-Zionist. "You are lying," he told me, and threw me out from his office. In the doorway, he told me that he doesn't want to ever see me in his office again.

Mazal Tov!

Years later, I learned that a member of the kibbutz had sent a letter to the American Consulate in Haifa. It stated that I didn't leave the kibbutz of my own volition; that I was thrown out because of my association with the Communist party. I can understand why the man wrote that letter. He was upset. He was my mentor, in a way. I probably undermined his resolve in politics.

Some 20 years later, while visiting Katka Frankova, in Israel, I met one of the members of the kibbutz, who also had left, years before. He told me that I was mistaken to think that he sent the letter.

"What letter?" I asked.

"The letter that was sent to the American Consulate in Haifa, claiming you were a Communist."

I told him that I had no idea that a letter was ever sent to the consul in Haifa. I also told him that I don't want to know who sent it.

In New York, my Uncle Harry hired a lawyer. He advised the family to apply for an immigration visa. Since my mother was an American citizen, and my step-father, a decorated veteran of World War II, the immigration office could not refuse to issue us a visa.

He was right!

Five years later I was called for an interview in the American Embassy in Tel-Aviv. I asked for an interpreter. The officer said my English was sufficient and no interpreter would be necessary. I won't describe the whole interview, but one episode is worthwhile mentioning. The officer asked me if I had participated in a theatrical show that was anti-American. I said, yes I did. "You played the roll of an American captain, did you?"

"Yes I did."

"There were parts in the show that were more or less anti-American?" I told him that I am an actor; I strive for the leading rolls and not for the supporting ones. He liked my answer.

182

"Now you talk like a capitalist," was his remark. Two years later, without any fanfare, I received a letter asking me to come to Tel Aviv to pick up the immigration visas for all my family.

Go figure!

ISRAEL STAGE TWO

Ella, my stepfather's sister, was very accommodating. For a change, I was in a complete dilemma. I was 25 years old, and under no circumstances would I agree to live off my mother's financial support, especially with a wife. At the time, I had two choices: Because I was a truck driver in the kibbutz, it would have been an easy task for me to get a bus driver's license. My Uncle Harry was ready to put down the necessary $5,000 at the time, to become a member in the Eged Bus Company. The other possibility was to become a welder. It was a good paying occupation. I wasn't a welder but I felt that I could bluff my way "with the help of some connections" into a well paying job. I hesitated becoming a bus driver, because while driving a truck, I started to have serious backaches. The welding job was something I could count on. It required union membership that was no more than hot air.

Alexander, Ella's husband, was a photographer. His studio was on Hertzel Street in Haifa. He suggested that while waiting to make up my mind, I should come to his studio and see if I would like to learn photography. I never held a camera in my hand before. I was never interested in the profession; not as a hobby, and surely not as a profession. It was a set-up, concocted by my mother and Alexander.

There had to be some financial agreement between Alexander and my mother. I was kept in the dark, for a good reason. My mother knew me well and suspected that I would not agree to be helped. I was a proud, stubborn, stupid, 25 year old, young man.

The studio was a five-man operation. Alexander's brother, Zoli Jakubovitz took care of the dark-room. I became his assistant. Zoli was a great guy. He was a veteran of World War II. He served as a tank driver in a Czech brigade. He was seriously injured; found bleeding next to his tank, and saved by his comrades. In 1948 he served in the Israeli army.

We hit it off from the first minute. From day one, he let me do the developing, soon to do the printing. My work was done under his careful supervision. Within six months, I worked independently. Here and there I had to ask for Zoli's help, but by and large, I handled the

184

work with required quality

Until then, I worked gratis. I thought the time had come to be paid as an apprentice.

I was paid.

After an additional four months, I got a raise. Little did I know where the money came from. If I had known that my mother was behind the ruse, I would have exploded, and would have never been a photographer.

Close to a year went by. I was happy with my advancement in the profession. I had no plans for the future. But with a stroke of luck, things changed.

The darkroom had no air-conditioning. There was a small ventilator next to the ceiling. It was an especially hot day; the small ventilator decided to quit. A repairman was called in. I struck up a conversation with him. It turned out to be that, Aaron Sobol, the repairman, was my neighbor.

Aaron was an enigma. He was of Polish, Jewish background. He studied medicine in Pisa, Italy. Because of the then fascist regime, he had to leave Italy. He moved to Paris, and applied to the Sorbonne. In Paris he couldn't get into medical school, so he signed up for engineering. Tough luck chased Aaron in Paris. He was conscripted into the French Army, and sent to Africa, where he went AWOL. How he got to Israel, then still Palestine, I don't know. One thing I knew: Aaron was blessed with all the brains in the world, but whoever doled out man's destiny, forgot to give him luck; whatever luck is. Aaron was married to Rozl, a baker's daughter, from a German, Jewish background; a sweet, happy-go-lucky lady. They had two children; a girl named Rina and a boy named Oded, Shay, another boy, was born later.

Aaron had an unusual talent for languages. He spoke, read, and wrote, Polish, Yiddish, Hebrew, German, French, Italian, and English.

He was ten years my senior. He was the brightest, wittiest man I ever met. He became my mentor. He drove me crazy. You have to go to school, you have to study, you won't be anything without an education. It became a daily refrain. I got sick of the pressure. I agreed, in principle, to look for a school of photography, There were none in Israel at that time.

Aaron remembered a school of photography in Paris. Without

my knowledge, he started to make inquiries. As soon as he received the first letter from the school, he told me to start taking French lessons. I thought the whole idea was pretty crazy. I didn't take the request for French language studies seriously. But not Aaron; he was dead serious.

In no time, he received an invitation, in my name, to come to Paris, to take a required test. The school in Paris required two years of art school, preferable on a university level, and two additional years of experience in photography. I had 5 years of junior high. That didn't disturb Aaron. He wrote to the school, that because I was educated in Czechoslovakia, all the documents were lost when the school burned down during the war. Additionally, there were restrictions to get a student visa from Israel. The consulate will issue a visa only if there is an invitation by a legitimate school and money deposited in a French bank. The beautiful letters Aaron wrote must have impressed the admissions officer, because without further correspondence, I was accepted in the Ecole.

As I mentioned before, I never thought that the plan to study photography in Paris will ever come to fruition; therefore I didn't bother with my French lessons. I had two months to cram in as much French as possible. It wasn't easy.

The day arrived to go to the French consulate to pick up the visa. Because I had all the necessary papers in order, I thought that the visit will be only a formality.

Was I wrong!

The consul met me in the front office. He asked in what language I would prefer the interview; French or English. What interview? I am not looking for a role in a French movie. I was stunned. My mind raced a mile a minute. My knowledge of French was hardly 100 words. In English, maybe a little bit more. I chose English. I was ushered into the consul's office. He settled behind his desk and started with a barrage of questions. I couldn't pick up a single word. Not even an "is" or an "and." Because of his accent, I thought he was speaking French. In my limited French, I told him. "Monsieur. Je nes comprend pas Fracais mais je parle Anglaise."

"Je parle Anglaise." was his answer. And he kicked me out of his office.

What am I going to do? I was supposed to be in Paris the next month. I called Aaron in utter panic. What am I going to do? He told

186

me not to worry. He asked me to calm down. In the next 24 hours he will have a solution to my problems. The next day, he had a solution. I had to travel to Vienna, where the French consulate issued visas to Israelis, without delay.

Great!

In the morning, I was on my way to Tel-Aviv. There was no Austrian Consulate in Haifa. At the Austrian Consulate, I was to claim that there was an exhibition of photographic equipment in Vienna and that I am interested in opening a studio in Israel and want to buy the necessary equipment. It was an invention of Aaron's imagination.

As we waited for our passports to be stamped with the Austrian visa, I observed two young women filling out a questionnaire. The younger of the two wore a military uniform with the rank of captain. The older one wore civilian clothes. I forgot that scene until my wife Anita, and I were sitting in the dining room of a ship sailing to Naples.

The two ladies that I had seen at the Austrian consulate were now sitting at the table next to ours. I suddenly recalled the scene in the Austrian consulate. As is customary in Israel, where everybody talks to anybody, I turned to the ladies and greeted them with the usual "shalom." The older of the two turned around and asked me if I know her. I answered in the positive. "Where do you know me from?" she asked.

"I won't tell you. You will have to guess." I said. She quoted some 10, maybe more, places. The answer was always, "no." There were two empty seats at our table, so I suggested that the ladies join us and I will divulge the secret of my knowledge. To make the story short, we hit it off. We had a good laugh and continued to see each other for the next three days of our voyage.

A young man, in an American military uniform, boarded the ship with two French beauties. One of our companions, the older one, (I won't mention her name) fell coo-coo for the American and coaxed him to join us. That's how we became a group of five. Tova, the older, turned out to be, to the best of my knowledge, a high ranking officer in the Ladies Air Force, though not in uniform when we first met, and Hanna, the younger, was her adjutant. They were on their way to a vacation in Italy and Austria.

The American was Alfred Kohn. In Naples, he took over our

relationship. He found a place in a small hotel, where for one dollar, we were able to spend the night. In the middle of the night there was a knock on the door; the police. We were in a hotel which also served the prostitutes. The police found three gals and two guys in one room. It took a lot of explanation. At the conclusion, with Alfred the American soldier, and a couple of packs of American cigarettes, things calmed down.

Next day we toured Naples. We took the train to Rome in the evening.

We arrived in Rome in the middle of the night. None of us spoke Italian. As we were talking to each other in Hebrew, a man passed by and inquired about our dilemma. He turned out to be a member of the Israeli consulate in Rome. He took the gals to a convent to spend the night. Alfred and I found a room in a hotel that turned out to be a bordello.

On one of the outings to Tivoli, we befriended a bunch of Indian students. One evening we met for pizza in a restaurant. The gals had a ball. The Indians went ga-ga for them. There must have been some 70 men and only one Indian lady. They were all students in the best schools in England and the USA.

Alfred departed Rome for Germany. The two Israeli ladies, and Anita and I, hung out for a few more days in Rome. From there we traveled to Florence. In Florence, all of us stayed in a youth hostel. The price was right. The charge for the night was 20 cents; 30 cents with a white sheet.

One evening, while sitting on the stairs of the youth hostel, eating a supper of bread and cheese, I struck up a conversation with an Austrian student. I told him that I am on my way to Paris to study photography.

"What a coincidence." he said. His girl friend was a good friend of the principal of the Graphishe Lehr and Versuhanstalt, the Institute of Photography, and she had just graduated from the school.

He thought that the school in Vienna was better than the one in Paris. He told me that it is very hard to be accepted, but if anybody can help me, his girlfriend, because of her close relationship with the principal, can.

"Take her telephone number, call her when you are in Vienna." he told me. My first reaction was, that's crazy, I am not going to study in Vienna, I am going to Paris. I didn't want to take the address of his girlfriend. Somehow he took a piece of paper, wrote down her name and telephone number, and stuffed it in my pocket.

From Florence, we traveled to Venice. The youth hostel in Venice could not compare with our experience in other Italian cities. It was clean and comfortable. True a little more expensive. Sixty cents didn't make a big hole in our pockets.

We traveled to Vienna from Florence. There we said goodbye to Tova and Hanna.

A small incident, worthwhile mentioning, happened on the train from Florence to Vienna. The four of us had third class tickets. We were always late. This time was no exception. All seats in third class were occupied. Some wise guy told us that if there are no empty seats in third class we can travel in second class. And if second class is filled we should look in the first class section of the train. Not bothering further, all four of us settled in the first class. The two girls, Tova, Hana, and my wife, Anita, got seats, but I sat on my valise in the compartment isle. The conductor, an Italian man, didn't agree with our contention. He asked for additional funds. Tova, the spokeslady of the group, argued with the conductor.

Not to confuse the situation, she spoke to the conductor in Hebrew. Everybody had a good laugh. It seemed that the conductor felt insulted and tried to remove the girls by force. That didn't sit well with me. I grabbed him by his collar, called him a Fascist, and punched him in the nose. A minute later, two Italian carabiniere grabbed me, and took me off the train. Lucky for us, a musician from Vienna, who traveled with us, and spoke Italian, took our side, and the whole thing turned to singing and drinking with the Italian carabiniere, all the way to Udine.

FIRST DAY IN VIENNA

We checked into a hotel in Vienna. The Austrian student in Florence had given me his girl friend's telephone number. What made me call the girl, I don't really know. It took years to find an explanation. Most probably I felt that my knowledge of German was much superior to French. To make the story short, I put in a call to the unknown female. She was very friendly; her boyfriend, the Austrian student, must have tipped her off, because she sounded as though she anticipated the call. In less than half an hour, she called back and told me to see the school principal the next morning. A student in the class had quit and there was now an opening.

My wife spoke fluent German. She accompanied me to the interview. She did all the talking. Jestingly, the principal asked if I planned to bring her to class. He told me I shouldn't be concerned because a Viennese born Israeli is in the class and he will help me to learn German. His name was David Ehrenfeld. I owed him a lot. I lost track of David. Every time I am in Israel I try to find him. So far to no avail.

We rented a furnished room, a couple of blocks from the school. The landlady lived with her daughter and a parrot called Vicki. She was a strange bird. Signs were put up on the kitchen door to close it so Vicki wouldn't catch cold. On the toilet door was a reminder to flush after using. Did Vicki drink from the toilet? We paid no attention. The price was right. We could come and go at any hour of day or night.

The class had only 12 students: three women and nine men. There was one Swedish guy, named Hasselstrom, David and I, the Israelis, and the rest were all Austrians. With David's help I was able to follow the lectures. After three months into the semester, I took my first test. I passed with flying colors. From there on it was smooth sailing. I finished on top of the class in photography and second place overall; behind Mueller, one of the Austrians. I don't remember her first name.

I had a friendly relationship with all my fellow students. Hasselstrom introduced me to horse racing, and Frankhauser, to drinking. Frankhauser's drinking was the result of the war. He was a Wehrmacht soldier, captured by Yugoslav partisans, and worked as a cook for two years, in the mountains of Serbia.

It had been 10 years since the Nazis were defeated, but some uneasiness lingered in the air. Nothing overt, but one could feel a certain uneasiness in facing each other. One of the professors teaching color photography, did needle me. He lost a leg in the war. He was a bitter, young man. I held back, not because I wanted to. I didn't want to create a situation that would disturb the class. One day I felt that he crossed the line. I told him, "You know, professor, what's wrong with you? Pity you didn't loose your other leg." It was an ugly, stupid thing to say, but he asked for it. And I wasn't going to apologize.

Not to a Nazi!

I got a "C" in color photography. I wasn't in the school collecting good marks. I was there to learn a profession. And learn I did!

We joined the club of Israeli students. Most were studying medicine. David and I were in photography, and one studied business. Three local Jewish kids hung around in the club. Two brothers and a young kid named Loisi Husser. Loisi invited us to his house. He introduced us to his sister, Andrea, and his parents. They lived in a villa in the outskirts of Vienna. The Hussers had a factory in Vienemeustadt, and a summer home on the Danube.

The father and mother were very happy that their children had Jewish company and to assure the connection, they treated us like celebrities. We were invited to the best restaurants. In particular, I remember a restaurant called the Kertzen Stuberl. We dined in a separate room at candle light; three waiters serving six people, with gypsies playing Hungarian tunes. New Year's Eve they took us to a Viennese ball. Mrs. Husser wore a long gown. Mr. Husser wore tails with all the military decoration of World War I. Andrea wore a white dress. She was a debutante. Loisi wore a tuxedo.

I didn't venture to the dance floor because I didn't own a tux.

The opera house had opened after 10 years of restoration. The opening afternoon concert was Beethoven's Ninth Symphony, conducted by Bruno Walter.

It was a once in a lifetime experience.

In the National Theatre, we were lucky to see Werner Kraus and a very young Oskar Werner, appearing in Schiller's Torquato

Tasso. We attended more than 70 performances; standing, because I had no money to buy good tickets.

In June 1956, we took a train to Naples, and there we boarded the ship on our way back to Israel. My wife, Anita, was in her sixth month of pregnancy. On November 13, 1956, our son was born. We named him Oded.

Anita and I were divorced in 1984.

Oded now lives in Colorado with his wife, Betty-Ann and their three children; the twins Jason and Eric, and the little guy, Ian.

I am now married to my big love from Israel, Katka Frankova.

Letter from John Lundgren
To Gabi Ron:

I sat down to read your manuscript last night. After I started, I could not put it down. Although the parts of your life before the Nazis intruded were certainly entertaining, your early years, various pranks, playing soccer, relationships with friends and relatives, wry comments on your Hebrew education, etc, it somehow seems offensive for me to say that I enjoyed it. How can someone "enjoy" reading about such a disaster as WWII and the Holocaust? Nevertheless, you infuse your writing with such a spirit that your story becomes compelling, commands the reader's attention, and demands to be read from start to finish. At least that was my experience. Hats off to you for making the effort to preserve, in writing, a story that should not be forgotten.

Anyone can list a sequence of events, dates, and places, and mistakenly believe such a list is the story of his or her life. What we really want to know, what brings the story to life, are the writer's thoughts and reflections on those events, dates, and places. I especially liked (enjoyed?) your running commentary throughout your manuscript, never mincing words, where you stand back from your narrative to point out the ludicrousness, the ironies, and the insanity of so much of what happened to you before you were sixteen years old. It starts immediately with your opening line: "In the beginning, whatever!" lots of symbolism and hidden meaning in those few words, the foreshadowing of your views on religion to mention just one.

Of the statements or ideas, I would have to include your leitmotiv of "free will" that reoccurs throughout your story, how you did not ask to be born, yet still had to suffer the consequences. "How smart was it to bring a child into this world (1938) without consulting the one who has to face the music?" Your sense of humor radiates from every page, too numerous to mention (except a few at the bottom.) Many other parts of your text are ripe for hours of discussion which, of course, is beyond the scope of this e-mail. The following are a few of those more profound statements:

"The time and effort I put in to memorize all those prayers and blessings I could have mastered calculus."

"Lots of Jews burned in hell, but not because they picked up a stone on Saturday or watched the priest blessing the congregation, or even eating pork."

"One can always use his imagination not to offend God."

"He (the teacher) would send a message to my father...complimenting me on my math test, but adding that the Jews are good in math because they are money lenders."

"If anyone can imagine hell, this was it."

"There was never a love affair between the Polish and Hungarian Jews...Only the Nazis were biased?"

"I am the recipient of A-10490. There was no need for names anymore."

"I am not sure about the crime I committed. I don't remember being in court. On the other hand, I must have committed some heinous crime. People don't get sentenced to death just like that!"

"I thought there must be some mitigating circumstances. My hair was lighter than Adolf's, my eyes are green. I don't have a hooked nose."

"Stefen was a Mensch." (Ein hoher kompliment, wenn man deutsch richtig versteht was das Wort, Mensch, bedeutel; schwer auf englisch to uebersetzen."

"Whatever happened, an SS could always blame the Jew."

"True, it was a sunny day; the skies were blue, only a small cloud lingered over Birkenau, and the always present smell of burning flesh." (The contrast is profound.)

"Shma Israel! Oh hear Yea Israel, we are duped! Maybe we duped ourselves!"

"What would Rabbi Jungreis say? Would he stick to his anti-Zionist ideas? How would he explain the absence of divine intervention?"

"I got even! I got even with a horse! Go figure!"

"At the end, Ervin and I survived. Bandi wasn't that lucky, fate, destiny, luck? Go figure!" (Some luck to be sure, but your youth, your physical conditioning, your smaller stature needing fewer calories, and, above all, your indomitable spirit certainly contributed.)

"Sometimes ten or more cigarettes could purchase a loaf of

bread. A hundred made one a millionaire…"

I did not realize at the time that to survive a certain time in the camp gave one a certain status "…As strange as it sounds, after a while a relationship developed between the guards and us." (Perhaps after a few months you were no longer just a number, but a real person, someone whose personality they knew, which inhibited at least some of the guards from mistreating you?)

"At the time, Germany conscripted children to protect the Third Reich from the Russians and the Americans. Here (in the camp) able bodied young SS were fighting the International Jew. What a formidable army of Jews they had to face!"

"…dressed in designer pajamas with clogs to match…" (Your sense of humor must have helped you survive. More examples below.)

"The cattle cars were ready and now the second time in a year I was traveling on the expense of the Third Reich."

"The tattoos were not enough for the Mauthausen authorities. They had their own accounting firm."

"We were not surprised when we were told to pack…We the striped ones had nothing to pack. We always traveled light."

"There was no welcoming sign at the gate." (a wry reference to the customary "Arbeit Macht Frei!" greeting.)